# THE REPUBLIC OF CHINA IS ON THE MOVE

# THE REPUBLIC OF CHINA IS ON THE MOVE

President Chiang Ching-Kuo's first
year in office shapes the policies
that will decide the nation's destiny

Kwang Hwa Publishing Co.
October 1979

Printed in Taiwan,
Republic of China
Kwang Hwa Publishing Co.
1-3, Chunghsiao E. Road,
Taipei, Taiwan
Republic of China

The Republic of China is alive and well despite a decade of buffeting that extended from loss of United Nations membership to the U.S. recognition of the Chinese Communists. As President Chiang Ching-kuo completed his first year at the helm on May 19, 1979, Free China had successfully weathered the severance of U.S. diplomatic relations and was doing as well as any country in the world to protect the 17 million people of Taiwan against the erosion of inflation and the energy shortage.

President Chiang said he was an optimist. That sounded the keynote of the Republic of China and its people in their approach to both international and domestic problems. Substantial relations are still maintained with the United States and all other states of the anti-Communist and non-Communist world. Trade with these countries will be close to US$30 billion this year on a two-way basis. Per capita income is climbing toward the US$2,000 mark. Defense self-sufficiency is increasing. In all Asia, there is no more politically stable land than the Republic of China on Taiwan.

Nominated by the Kuomintang, Chiang Ching-kuo (then the Premier of the Republic of China) was elected President by the National Assembly March 21 to succeed President Yen Chia-kan, who had asked that he not be considered to succeed himself and urged the nomination and election of Premier Chiang. President Yen said Premier Chiang was uniquely qualified to lead the nation through difficult times and complete the tasks of anti-Communism and national recovery.

President Chiang Ching-kuo was born in Chekiang province, in 1910. He is married and has three sons and a daughter. His father sent him to Moscow to school when he was 16 years old. He attended Sun Yat-sen University there. His career in government administration began in 1939 during the War of Resistance Against Japan. He was appointed Administrative Commissioner of southern Kiangsi province and held that post until 1945. As the war ended, he became Foreign Affairs Commissioner for Northeast China (1945-47). The Communist rebellion was mounting in tempo when he was made Deputy Economic Control Supervisor in 1948. He tried to stabilize the economy and cracked down on profiteers and black marketing.

The first Taiwan assignment of Chiang Ching-kuo was as chairman of the Kuomintang Provincial Headquarters in 1949-50. From 1950 to 1954 he was director of the General Political Warfare Department of the Ministry of National Defense. He served concurrently as a member of the Kuomintang Reform

President Chiang Ching-kuo received a high-ranking U.S. delegation led by the deputy secretary of state, Warren Christopher, third from left, after President Carter announced the break in diplomatic relations with the Republic of China as of Jan. 1, 1979.

Committee from 1950 to 1952. He was chairman of the Vocational Assistance Commission for Retired Servicemen from 1957 to 1964 and then Deputy Minister of National Defense in 1964 and 1965. He was Deputy Secretary General of the National Defense Council from 1954 to 1967. He was Minister Without Portfolio for a time and is a member of the Standing Committee of the Central Committee of the Kuomintang.

Before his election, President Chiang Ching-kuo traveled abroad as a representative of the President, the government and the people of the Republic of China. He visited the United States in 1953, 1963, 1965, 1969 and 1970. He met with President John F. Kennedy in 1963. President Lyndon B. Johnson in 1965 and President Richard Nixon in 1970. In 1969 he attended the funeral services for President Dwight D. Eisenhower, whom he had known both in the United States and Taiwan. Other travels have taken him to Japan, South Korea and Thailand.

The period from May 20, 1978, to May 19, 1979, was one of the most eventful in Free China's history. On December 16 of 1978 (Taipei time), President Jimmy Carter announced that his administration had decided to recognize the Chinese Communists and sever diplomatic relations with the Republic of China as of January 1, 1979. He also announced that as of the same date, the Republic of China would be given one year's notice of U.S. intention to sever the Mutual Defense Treaty of 1954.

In his inaugural address May 20, 1978, President Chiang had said that strengthening of the U.S. relationship was the consistent policy and principle of the Republic of China. "Anything which benefits China will also benefit the United States and anything which harms China will also harm the United States," the President said. "If the two countries stick together, both will benefit; if they are separated, both will suffer." Any move toward appeasement of or coexistence with the Chinese Communists would confront the free nations with the dilemma of "battling a tiger at the front door" while "letting a wolf in through the back door," he added.

The people of Free China replied to President Carter's unilateral breaking of formal relations with an outburst of patriotic fervor. At marches and rallies, tens of thousands gave generously to a national defense fund which subsequently raised more than NT$3 billion. Overseas Chinese communities pledged their support. In a statement to the people and nation, the President said:

"The decision by the United States to establish diplomatic relations with the Chinese Communist regime has not only seriously damaged the rights and interests of the government and people of the Republic of China, but also has had tremendous adverse impact upon the entire free world. For all the consequences that might arise as a result of this move, the government of the United States alone should bear the full responsibility.

"In the last few years, the U.S. government has repeatedly reaffirmed its assurances to maintain diplomatic relations with the Republic of China and to honor its treaty commitments. Now that it has broken the assurances and abrogated the treaty, the U.S. government cannot be expected to have the confidence of free nations in the future.

"The U.S. extension of diplomatic recognition to the Chinese Communist regime, which owes its very existence to

Taiwan produces a
surplus of rice and
storing it with minimum
loss is important.
This is the godown of
a Farmers' Association
in the Pingtung area
of the south. The
government is pledged
to buy excess stocks.

terror and suppression, is not in conformity with her professed position of safeguarding human rights and strengthening the capabilities of the democratic nations so as to resist the totalitarian dictatorships. Such a move is tantamount to denying the hundreds of millions of enslaved people on the Chinese mainland of their hope for an early restoration of freedom. Viewed from whatever aspect, the move by the United States constitutes a great setback for human freedom and democratic institutions. It will be condemned by all freedom-living and peace-loving peoples of the world.

"Recent international events have proven that the U.S. pursuance of the 'normalization' process with the Chinese Communist regime did not protect the security of free Asian nations; it has further encouraged Communist subversion and aggressive activities and hastened the fall of Indochina into Communist hands. The government and people of the Republic of China firmly believe lasting international peace and security can never be established on an instable foundation of expediency.

"Regardless of how the international situation may develop, the Republic of China as a sovereign nation will, with her glorious tradition, unite all her people, civilian and military, at home and abroad, to continue her endeavors of progress in social, economic and political fields. The Chinese government and people, faithful to the national objectives and their international responsibilities, have full confidence in the future of the Republic of China.

"The late President Chiang Kai-shek repeatedly instructed the Chinese people to be firm with dignity and to complete the task of national recovery and national reconstruction. The government and people of the Republic of China have determination and faith that they will extert their utmost to work together with other free peoples in democratic countries and counter Communist tyrannical rule and aggressive policy. Henceforth, we shall be calm and firm, positive and hardworking. It is urged that all citizens cooperate fully with the government, with one heart and one soul, united and determined to tide over this difficult moment. Under whatever circumstances, the Republic of China will neither negotiate with the Chinese Communist regime nor compromise with Communism, and will never give up her sacred tasks of recovering the mainland and delivering the compatriots there. This firm position will not be changed."

Premier Y.S. Sun and other ranking members of the government reported to President Chiang on the nation's

strength and determination. The Premier said: "We can have confidence in overcoming any adverse situation ahead of us so long as we stand united and share fortune or misfortune with each other." He noted that the Republic of China had armed forces of half a million men plus 2.5 million reservists with modern weapons and training. Foreign exchange reserves of more than US$6 billion assured ample funds to buy advanced weapons system and increase the degree of defense self-sufficiency.

President Chiang Ching-kuo had worked long and valiantly to maintain the U.S. tie. Soon after his inauguration, he told David Reed, an editor of the *Reader's Digest,* that "our interests and those of America cannot be divided. If we go separate ways, both will suffer. In any case, the Republic of China will persist." He had expressed similar sentiments while visiting the United States. In 1970, while Vice Premier, Chiang Ching-kuo went to Washington as guest of the American government and was honored in a manner befitting a chief of state rather than a deputy prime minister. In an arrival statement, he said he had come to the United States "to add to the reservoir of friendship and understanding already existing between our two countries." He had an hour's private talk with President Nixon and was the guest of honor at a presidential dinner.

Top: Visiting a fishing boat at Suao on the east coast. Bottom: Three generations of a family at Hsinchu on the northwestern plain enjoy their unexpected meeting with the nation's chief executive.

11

Fruit growing is both a full-time occupation and a sideline of Taiwan's farmers. Although the concentration is on tropical varieties, pears and apples are grown on the slopelands of the Central Mountains. Many fruit farmers are retired soldiers.

Addressing a subsequent dinner meeting in New York, Chiang Ching-kuo said: "Our two nations are founded on faith — faith in our people, faith in our government, faith that the causes of freedom, justice and righteousness will prevail. The ideals of America are set forth in the preamble to a constitution that was ordained and established in the name of justice, domestic tranquillity, common defense, general welfare and the blessings of liberty. Chinese ideals are rooted in the teachings of Confucius and the other sages. These have found latter day expression in Dr. Sun Yat-sen's Three Principles of the People. Dr. Sun borrowed from your Abraham Lincoln for his assertion that the Principles of the People are to be implemented by a government of the people, by the people and for the people.

"Historically, our countries have had deep faith in each other. The United States never had predatory ambitions in China. The Open Door Policy is one of the great building blocks of your policy in Asia. America used her share of the Boxer indemnity to support Chinese students. China and the United States were firm and faithful allies in the Second World War and then joined with other free countries to write the Charter of the United Nations."

He went on to say that the Chinese Communists could not possibly survive, unless given a new lease of life by the free world and the United States. He called attention to the contrast between the good life of Taiwan and the impoverished life of the Chinese mainland. Speaking before the exodus of refugees had become a crisis, he said: "Thousands of refugees tell us what is in the hearts of the Chinese people. They tell this truth over and over, month after month and year after year."

President Chiang continued and enlarged the friendships and contacts of this and other American trips over a period of decades. While defense minister, he had come to know most of the U.S. military leaders. He had a role in negotiating the U.S.—ROC Mutual Defense Treaty signed in 1954. In June of 1978, President Chiang met with Edward W. Scripps II, vice president of the Scripps-Howard Newspapers, and commented on the treaty which President Carter said the United States is terminating. President Chiang said Secretary of State John Foster Dulles had correctly foreseen that the Chinese Communist regime was the enemy of the United States and intended to communize all of Asia. History, the President said, has shown that the Chinese Communists are not only the enemy of the United States but a threat to the security

Farm homes are comfortable and warm in the winter, cool in the summer. Most homes have a family altar. About a third of the 17 million people of Taiwan still live on farms or in villages adjacent to the fields.

of Southeast Asia and, for that matter, to the whole Asian region. Anticipating the Chinese Communist invasion of Vietnam, he added that the threat was steadily becoming more serious. The treaty, he said, not only benefits the Republic of China but is of great significance to the permanent interests of the United States.

In the same discussion, President Chiang made these four points regarding U.S. relations with the Chinese Communists:

First, the U.S. concept of checkmating Russia with the Chinese Communist regime is impractical. The United States should be careful to understand that the Chinese Communists are trying to make capital of the anti-Russian sentiments of Americans and that in the end they will try to push the United

States to the brink of war. The Chinese Communist design is to embroil the United States and Soviet Russia in a conflict which would cripple both and give the Peiping regime an opportunity to fish in troubled waters. The attempt to checkmate Russia with the Chinese Communist regime and the effort to strike a balance between Russia and the Chinese Communists amount to the walking of a tightrope—the greatest care is necessary to keep from falling into the abyss.

Second, the Chinese Communists turn a smiling face to the United States because the latter continues to maintain formal diplomatic relations with the Republic of China. Should the so-called "normalization of relations" with the Chinese Communists be carried out, the Peiping regime will no longer hold the United States in high regard and continue to make seemingly friendly advances. (These are words that have turned out to be prophetic.)

Third, the strategic position of Taiwan is vital to the basic fabric of American interests. In recent years, the Soviet Union has attempted to expand its influence in the seas of Eastern Asia. Russian naval vessels have been active from Vladivostok in the north to the Strait of Malacca in the south and have recently appeared in the Taiwan Straits. Russian expansion in this area constitutes a strategic threat to the United States. Americans should take this into consideration.

Fourth, the current U.S. approaches and efforts to please the Chinese Communists can achieve nothing. The Chinese Communists will laugh behind their masks and U.S. allies will lose their confidence in the Americans.

In November of 1978, President Chiang met with a 13-member U.S. Congressional delegation touring the Western Pacific. He told the group: "The national defense interests of the Republic of China are closely related to the national defense interests of the United States. To maintain and enhance stability in the region, the defense capability of the Republic of China must be strengthened, particularly through acquisition of high-performance aircraft. It is to be hoped that the United States understands this and will provide the planes."

After President Carter's announcement, the United States dispatched a 16-member mission headed by U.S. Deputy Secretary of State Warren Christopher to discuss the shape and details of the ongoing relationship between the Republic of China and the United States. President Chiang said that the future ties between the two countries must rest on the five principles of "reality, continuity, security, legality and govern-mentality." The chief executive explained the five principles

The ailing are not forgotten in the course of President Chiang's travels among the people. He stops at small rural hospitals and is especially solicitous of patients who have served in the armed forces. Taiwan's life span now averages 72 years.

Left: Warm handshakes with overseas Chinese tourists at Hualien on the scenic east coast. Right: Sampling sugar cane offered by touring students. The President has a special interest in young people, and likes to find out what visitors think about Free China.

as follows:

—The Republic of China is an independent sovereign state with a legitimately established government based on the Constitution of the Republic of China. It is an effective government which has the wholehearted support of her people. The international status and personality of the Republic of China cannot be changed merely because of the recognition of the Chinese Communists by any country of the world. The legal status and international personality of the Republic of China is a simple reality which the United States must recognize and respect.

—The United States has expressed its intention of continuing to maintain cultural, economic, trade, scientific, technological and travel relations with the Republic of China. The ties that bound our two countries and peoples together in the past, however, include much more than these. The Republic of China is ready and willing to continue these traditional ties. The United States, on the other hand, must also realize the importance of the continuity of these ties, not only in their present scope, but also on an expanded scale to meet future needs.

—The security of the Asian-Pacific region is also of utmost importance to the well-being and livelihood of the 17 million people on Taiwan, as well as American interests in the area. The Sino-U.S. Mutual Defense Treaty signed in 1954 was designed to be a vital link in the chain of the collective defense system of free countries in the Western Pacific. The situation in this region has not changed. It is still unstable and insecure.

Above: Learning the
trick of filling
and folding the Chinese
dumpling, one of
the tastiest snacks
in the cook's repertoire.
Right: Like other
Chinese, President
Chiang respects and
listens to the elderly.

The Republic of China refines its own oil and has been able to keep up with the rising demand for motor fuel and other forms of energy based on petroleum. At right, President Chiang exchanges greetings with a taxi driver at a Taipei filling station.

The threat of invasion and subversion by Communist forces to the free nations of Asia, particularly after the fall of Vietnam is even more serious than before.

—Hence, the U.S. unilateral action to terminate the Sino-U.S. Mutual Defense Treaty will further destabilize this region and might create a new crisis of war. Thus, in order to ensure the peace and security of the Western Pacific, which includes that of the Republic of China, it is imperative that the United States take concrete and effective measures to renew its assurances to countries in this region.

—The Republic of China is ready and determined to continue to do its share in securing stability and peace in the Western Pacific. But in order to do this, It must have sufficient capabilities to defend itself, and thereby protect its neighbors. President Carter has indicated that he is still concerned about the peace, security and prosperity of this region after the termination of the Sino-U.S. Mutual Defense Treaty and will continue to supply the Republic of China with defense weapons.

—The United States must give us assurances of a legal nature which would ensure the fulfillment of this commitment.

—The country is at present faced with the pragmatic problems involved in continuing and maintaining 59 treaties and agreements, as well as other arrangements, between our two countries. Since both the Republic of China and the United States are governed by law, the private interests of both Chinese and American citizens require the protection of definite legal provisions. Appropriate legislative measures in both countries must therefore be taken to provide a legal basis on which these security, commercial and cultural treaties and agreements can continue to remain in full force and effect.

—The complex nature of the activities of mutual interest to the two countries makes it impossible for them to be carried out by a private organization or individual. To facilitate the continuation and expansion of all relations between the two countries, it is necessary that government-to-government level mechanisms be set up in Taipei and Washington. This model alone can serve as the framework on which the future relationship of the two countries can be constructed.

In his New Year's (1979) message to the Chinese people, President Chiang said "our anti-Communist struggle will never cease until Communism is eliminated from Chinese territory and until the Chinese Communist regime has been destroyed. We are sure that any insurgent organization which runs contrary to the wishes and the will of the Chinese people and any evil force inconsistent with Chinese tradition will never be accepted

Memorial rallies and lectures are conducted regularly to further the teaching of Dr. Sun Yat-sen's Three Principles of the People. Like his father, President Chiang Kai-shek, the chief of state is a disciple of Dr. Sun.

After his inauguration
May 21, 1978, Presi-
dent Chiang greeted
visiting overseas
Chinese at the Chung-

shan Building atop
Yangmingshan in Taipei.
He told them he would
do his best to serve
the Chinese people
and assure a free
and united country.

or tolerated by the Chinese people and are bound to fail. Although the objective situation may sometimes follow a course unfavorable to us, we must carry on our struggle to final victory."

The nation's leader said that country "is again distressed and assaulted by adversity. But our ancient sages have told us that a country thrives on distress. We can see today that all of our compatriots at home and abroad have demonstrated with one will and one heart their absolute unity and patriotism. They have manifested our intrepid national founding spirit to the full. This attests that we can truly be firm with dignity and persevere with fortitude. This also attests that we can grow despite distress. So long as we maintain our confidence and the revolutionary vigor and fortitude that obtained at the time

Yangmingshan gets a new tree with the President's help on March 12, 1979, the anniversary of Dr. Sun Yat-sen's death in 1925, a date observed as Arbor Day by the people of the Republic of China.

of our national founding, we can cope with any challenge, stand up under any test, overcome any difficulty and surmount any barrier on the way to success."

Interviewed by René Viénet of the news magazine *L'Express* of Paris January 2, President Chiang said the United States had no reason to abrogate the Mutual Defense Treaty unilaterally. "The United States is known for its tradition of safeguarding freedom and human rights," he said. "I want to ask why the United States chose to establish diplomatic relations with Red China just as people the world over were accusing the Chinese Communists of killing many innocent people, ravaging human rights and depriving people of their freedom. I also want to ask why the United States should have decided to 'normalize relations' with the Chinese Communists at a time when people on the mainland are putting up posters to demand the restoration of their freedom. The United States claims to practice democracy and promote the rule of law. Why should President Carter betray us so soon after Congress had passed a resolution expressing the attachment of great importance to the ROC-U.S. defense treaty? The United States always hopes its allies will implement democracy. Then why did the United States announce its decision on recognizing the Chinese Communist regime as we were preoccupied with elections for additional members of our central parliamentary organizations?"

The President expressed hope the United States would continue to supply the Republic of China with weapons. "In the face of the Chinese Communist threat, we have always given first priority to the strengthening of our national defenses," he said. "We have continued to modernize our weapons and other defense equipment. Under these new circumstances, we certainly shall continue to modernize our weapons. We need better and faster planes and vessels to strengthen our sea and air defenses. In the past, we have ceaselessly tried to procure the most modern weapons from the United States but failed to get all that we wanted. To ensure Taiwan's security, it is the future responsibility of the United States to sell us the latest and most sophisticated weapons."

On February 15, the government announced the establishment of the Coordination Council for North American Affairs to carry on relations with the United States. The Americans named the American Institute in Taiwan as their counterpart to CCNAA. President Chiang addressed the following statement to the free Chinese people:

—The unilateral announcement of the U.S. government

Overseas Chinese are ardent backers of the Republic of China's cause. President Chiang Ching-kuo has an open door for those returning on the National Day and for other occasions of special importance.

Economic thinking of President Chiang calls for the development of industry without any neglect of the farm sector. Here he is briefed on Taiwan-made machinery at an export exhibition conducted in Taipei.

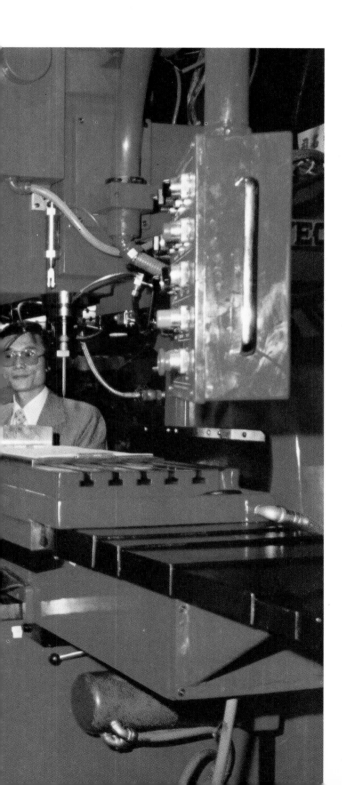

last December 15 terminating diplomatic relations with us and recognizing the tyrannical Chinese Communists was a historic tragedy affecting the whole world. In the last two months, we have endured the heavy pain in our hearts in order to negotiate and talk with the United States amidst danger and concern. We wanted to do all we could to mitigate damage from the tragedy and protect the interest of the country and people. In this period, we have done everything we could to carry out our country's fundamental policy. We especially appreciate the support of our compatriots at home and abroad. From beginning to end, they have trusted and encouraged the government and have contributed their wisdom and assistance to the country. We also have been deeply moved by the voice of justice persistently heard in the U.S. Congress and among the multitudes of the American people. This voice has given us warm sympathy and support. It has expressed the profound friendship between the peoples of the Republic of China and the United States and at the same time has indicated that justice still prevails.

—In order to restructure and seek the continued development of relations between our two countries, we have decided to set up a new organization. Reality requires that this time-honored and extremely close relationship be perpetuated, so we must swallow the bitter pill and handle the situation with all the fortitude at our command. We are also showing the Chinese people's ability to overcome extreme hardship with maximum courage and perseverance. As the negotiations between the two countries proceed, I must emphasize to all the people of the nation that the Republic of China's fundamental policy of anti-Communism and national recovery will never be changed. Current difficulties can in no way shake our confidence and determination. On the contrary, we shall execute our national policy more vigorously, courageously and determinedly. Politically, we shall remain in the democratic camp and safeguard human rights. Economically, we shall strengthen our construction program to sustain steady growth. Militarily, we shall fortify national defense to ensure national security. As long as we remain unafraid, do what we should, maintain our optimism and self-confidence and uphold our position with self-reliance, we can turn adversity to our advantage, open up a fresh vista and create a new horizon.

—With the weighty mandate of the people and in the face of national danger and difficulty, I have steadfastly urged myself to proceed with caution and courage and have never allowed myself the illusion that I can afford a single moment

Sales of whole plants, especially in Southeast Asia, have given a big boost to the machinery industry. The President has often noted the defense contributions of manufacturers and encouraged them.

Workers are the heart
of industry, and the
President loses no
opportunity to meet
with them and ask
about their problems.
The Ford-Lio Ho plant
at Chungli is one of
the biggest of a grow-
ing auto industry.

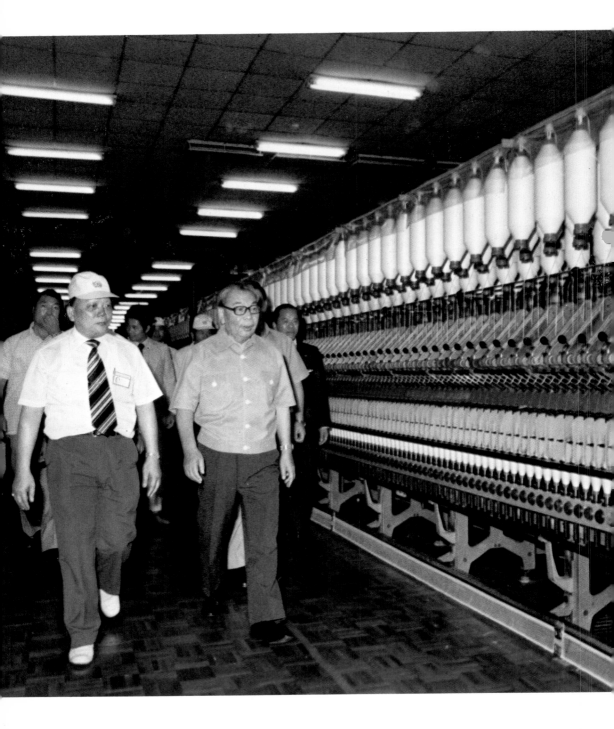

Textiles is the biggest Taiwan export industry and also a major supplier of the domestic market. Plants are modern and working conditions are good. This artificial fiber textile mill is at Taoyuan west of Taipei. Workers are pleased to see the President.

of negligence or laxity. I appreciate wholeheartedly the people's total and unreserved support of the government. I want to pledge anew that I shall contribute all that I have and join with my compatriots in partaking of both joy and sorrow. I shall unite with them indestructibly to carry out our common ideal and reach our common goal. We must march forward together courageously until we have won the final victory.

On March 20, President Chiang approved the purchase of 18 F5E jet fighters for the Self-Reliance Air Force Squadron. The planes will be paid for by the contributions of the people to the Self-Reliance and National Salvation Fund. Formal presentation of the planes to the Air Force is scheduled for the Double Tenth National Day this year.

The chief executive told Benno Kroll of the West German magazine *GEO* that the Republic of China does not rely entirely on military power for victory over the Chinese Communists. He said: "The late President Chiang Kai-shek pointed out that the mainland could be recovered through efforts that were '70 per cent political and 30 per cent military.' We do not rely completely on military strength to recover the mainland. We are building in Taiwan a democratic and free society based on the Three Principles of the People, and our accomplishments will have a significant political impact on the people of the mainland. The Chinese Communists seek to perpetuate their rule through totalitarian persecution and this has earned them the bitter hatred of all the people. Therefore, our effort to recover the mainland is in fulfillment of the people's wish. Any action that helps the mainland people eliminate tyrannical Chinese Communist control and the few Chinese Communist leaders will receive enthusiastic support from the mainland people and will not lead to world war."

President Chiang explored the political and psychological position of the Republic of China in depth during the course of his April 20 address to a Sun Yat-sen Memorial Service. He said: "For all Chinese, December 16, 1978, is an unforgettable date. This was a day that brought trauma to our hearts and made us realize the necessity of striving to the utmost for

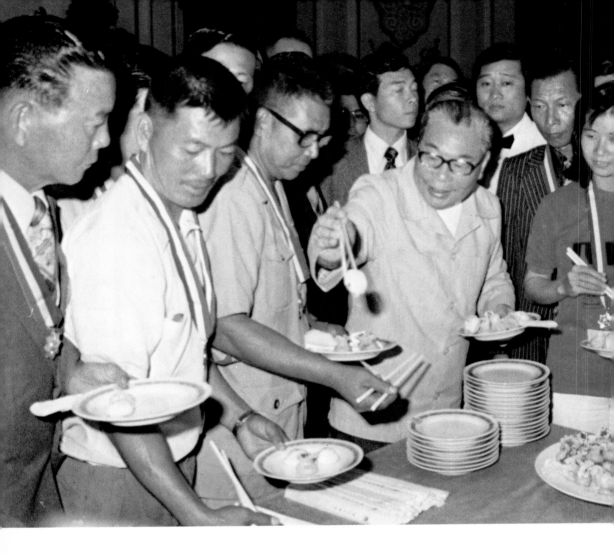

self-reliance. The shock to our hearts resulted from the actions of the government of the United States, leader of the free world, in mistaking an enemy for a friend and establishing diplomatic relations with the Chinese Communists, who have illegally occupied the Chinese mainland for 30 years, massacred a countless number of people and posed a continuous threat to world peace. At the same time, the United States severed diplomatic relations with the Republic of China, a cooperative friend of long standing, a faithful ally bound to the U.S. by a mutual defense treaty and steadfast combatant in the battle for freedom. What has happened is agonizing and dismaying. We have been compelled to strive steadily harder to achieve self-reliance in a world situation which is so difficult and treacherous. Now we can perceive the true meaning of the late President Chiang Kai-shek's instruction. The late President told us that 'under all conditions only our own strength is real strength' and that 'we must lay the foundations of any enterprise for ourselves and also resolve all the problems involved by ourselves.' As a consequence, we have never been depressed nor discouraged. To the contrary, we have become more determined than ever to brace up and continue the struggle for national survival and the development of our people.

Model workers are honored on Labor Day, May 1, and the President is on hand to extend congratulations and share the repast. Above, he exchanges greetings with engineers engaged in construction of the Chiang Kai-shek International Airport.

"Once diplomatic relations had been severed, the two countries conducted negotiations which had no parallel of struggle or substance in the history of diplomacy. We were completely aware that the negotiation environment was ominous in the extreme. But we had no choice except to restrain ourselves, enduring humiliation and 'upholding our target and holding our temper in check,' so as to make sure of attaining our national goal. We were deeply aware of the heavy burden that rested on our shoulders, yet realized that we had to exert ourselves and overcome all difficulties in the national interest. Our only choice was to take up the burden courageously and endure all hardships in order to protect the lives, freedom and happiness of the 17 million people in this bastion of national revival, and at the same time help our hundreds of millions of compatriots on the mainland throw off the yoke of Communist tyranny and come to enjoy with us a life of freedom and happiness. This is an immense responsibility involving the destiny of generation upon generation of the Chinese people. It is necessary that we have unconquerable determination and spirit in order to endure the humiliation and hardship and take up the burden and fulfill our task. Thus our enduring of humiliation is by no means a sign of cowardice or weakness. Rather, it is a manifestation of courage and fortitude. At the same time, our endurance of humiliation also has a limit, because we know that only when the Republic of China stands erect—upright and firm—can the peace and stability of East Asia be assured. We have therefore adhered steadfastly to the five negotiation principles of 'continuity,' 'reality,' 'security,' 'legality' and 'governmentality.' We did so for the common interests of the two countries and the happiness of Asia and the whole world. We have accepted this virtue as our burden and tried hard to minimize the hurt to open a new page in the book of history. In this time we should serve as witnesses of history and also as its creators.

"During the last four months, many developments seem to have promised major apocalyptical imprints for future history.

"First, our people at home and abroad have shown their soaring patriotism and wholehearted support of the government with enthusiastic and touching deeds. Scene after scene of moving stories have coalesced into page upon page of a patriotic panorama revealing the unanimous anti-Communist determination of the Chinese people and attesting that the tighter the crunch of the moment, the more solidly united are the people in showing the invincible spirit of the Chinese race.

Suao Harbor (top) and Taichung Harbor (bottom) are making major contributions to Taiwan trade and transportation. President Chiang has made frequent trips to both ports to encourage those who are engaged in construction work.

If young people are being honored, the President will not be far away. He undertook establishment of the China Youth Corps at the request of his father, President Chiang Kai-shek, and remained its chairman for several years. He has 3 sons, 1 daughter.

"Second, the U.S. Congress and huge numbers of Americans have extended to us their unparalleled warm friendship and massive support, providing unmistakable evidence that justice is always to be found in the hearts of the people and that the relationship between the Republic of China and the United States is indivisible. We are deeply appreciative and increasingly confident that ties between the two countries will be further developed and made even stronger.

"We can also see that during this same period our enslaved compatriots on the mainland have surged like winds and clouds to cry out for freedom, democracy, jobs and especially for the emulation of Taiwan. This anti-Communist uproar, which has been swelling up in the hearts of our mainland compatriots for years, is convincing evidence that they are hungry for liberty and prosperity and that they have maintained their allegiance to our government. These developments also show the great influence that the bastion of national revival on Taiwan, Penghu, Kinmen and Matsu is exercising over changes in the mainland situation. . .

"Looking over the world situation, we are certain that the pivotal position of the Republic of China is even more important than at any time in the past. The Chinese people on the mainland are sure that Communism is going to fall. They are disenchanted with Chinese Communist hypocrisy and deception and have lost all their illusions about the regime. They have come to understand that the existence of the Republic of China represents the hope of achieving China's destiny. Their only aspiration is to see the strength that they observe in our bastion of national recovery employed in the early recovery of the mainland. Under such circumstances, we must clench our teeth, endure any further buffeting, stand firm and break through any adverse tide by continuing our endeavors to make the country more powerful and our strength

President Chiang knows the Army first-hand and is former minister of national defense. He often gets together with armed forces members and usually attends service academy graduation ceremonies.

greater in order to carry out the tasks that our mainland compatriots expect of us."

President Chiang told James D. Cary of the Copley News Service that the Chinese Communists "have written the goal of invading Taiwan into their constitution" and that "they may advance the timetable to externalize their internal turmoil." He said there would be no negotiations or contacts with the Chinese Communists. "Since the U.S. establishment of diplomatic relations with Peiping," he said, "the Chinese Communists have stepped up their 'peaceful unification' propaganda to attain a goal that cannot be attained by force. We shall not fall into the Chinese Communist trap. Negotiations also are proscribed by the necessity of providing democracy-loving Chinese at home and abroad and freedom-seeking compatriots on the mainland with a model for the reconstruction of China and to make sure no one concludes we have given up our struggle for freedom and democracy."

The Republic of China will never seek rapprochement with

the Soviet Union, the President said. Rather, the ROC "will adhere to its anti-Communist national policy, remain in the democratic camp and continue to make positive contributions to world peace and security based on moral courage and the spirit of justice. We shall strengthen total diplomacy, expand economic and technological cooperation with countries having diplomatic relations with us to further consolidate bilateral relations, and further develop economic, trade, cultural and other substantial relations through various channels with non-Communist countries having no diplomatic relations with us."

President Chiang predicted a continuation of power struggle on the Chinese mainland. He said: "More political turmoil is in prospect on the Chinese mainland whether Teng Hsiao-ping lives or dies. The power struggle among the higher-ups in Communist China, the conflicts and crises involved in implementing the four modernizations and the discontent of tens of millions of rusticated youths, coupled with demands for a higher standard of living from the broad masses of workers and farmers, will give rise to an anti-Communist tide on the mainland and fuel hopes for freedom, democracy and a better life. All this must lead to political turmoil."

On May 28, *Time* magazine featured an interview of Marsh Clark, its Hongkong correspondent, with President Chiang. Asked about the trauma of U.S. "normalization of relations" with the Chinese Communists, the President said: "We did everything possible to prevent that nightmare from actually taking place. The first task for us was to face the reality and to manage the crisis imposed upon the nation, especially the adverse effects on society. We had to do something to minimize the unfortunate consequences. In the past months we have been doing everything possible to strengthen this society—economically, socially, militarily and politically—and we have been taking every possible step to unite the country. We feel that only with internal solidarity can we meet the external blow. Aside from the steps that we have been taking to meet the challenge, we know that the Republic of China and the United States share many, many common interests and that people-to-people relations between our two countries will never be terminated."

Commenting on the defense situation and the Mutual Security Treaty, President Chiang said that the United States seems to need the treaty as much in 1979 as in 1954 when it was signed. "For the good of the United States as well as of the Republic of China," he said, "this treaty should be kept in

One unfailing destination for the President each summer is the Hill of Success, training ground of ROTC students near Taichung in central Taiwan. He also goes often to Air Force bases to check on the preparedness of the first line of defense.

Students enjoy the
sightseeing of Taiwan,
so President Chiang
is sure to meet many
young people in the
course of his travels.
Left: At the Hsitou
forest recreation cen-
ter. Right: At the
island's northern tip.

Scouting is highly regarded in the Republic of China. President Chiang visited the International Boy Scout Jamboree in 1978 and talked with many of those who came from abroad. Boy and Girl Scouts sponsor outings for high school youngsters.

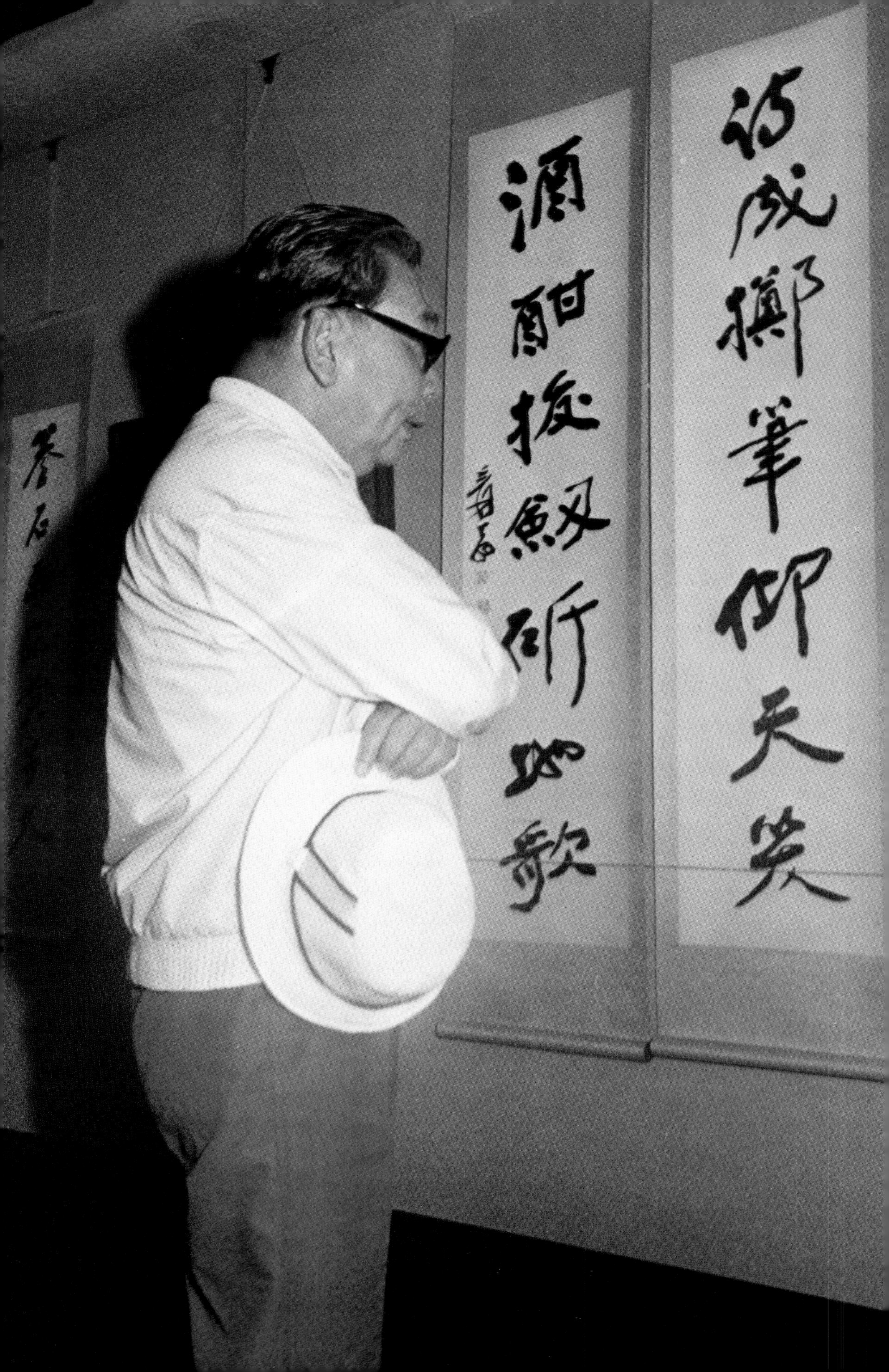
詩成擲筆仰天笑
酒酣拔劍斫地歌

effect. But President Carter has already announced his intention to terminate it at the end of this year. Now Congress has passed an act saying that the United States continues to be concerned about the security of the Republic of China. I think that's something that's necessary. The United States must remain concerned about the security and stability of the Republic of China because that is very important in terms of the U.S. strategic position in this part of the world. The purpose of the Mutual Defense Treaty was exactly in that context. I want to emphasize that when the Vietnam War was over, people talked about the so-called domino theory. If something serious happened in the Taiwan Straits and the U.S. lost its presence in this part of the world, then the damage to the security of the world would be much more serious than in the fall of Vietnam— and it would cause serious defense problems for Japan, the Philippines, Singapore and other countries in the region."

If the Chinese Communists launched an attack against the Republic of China, they would have to be prepared to pay the price of one, two or even three million lives, President Chiang said. He also emphasized the importance of politics in the ROC confrontation with the Chinese Communists. Many people on the mainland would oppose military action against Taiwan, he said, and this "would lead to the development of an anti-war movement and perhaps even a civil war." He viewed the Chinese Communist war with the Vietnamese as quite different from that between Peiping and the ROC. "When they took military action against Vietnam, the Chinese Communists could find many excuses to justify it," he said. "But if they go to war against us, they would have to have a very good reason. Also, Vietnam and China are contiguous by land, but when you talk about military action between the mainland and Taiwan, you must consider the natural barrier between us—the Taiwan Straits—which is 100 miles at its narrowest and 120 miles at the broadest points. If they undertake such amphibious action, it would be a very risky enterprise on their part. They would have to be prepared to sacrifice one million, two million or even three million people in that action. It would also involve a great logistical and transport problem for them."

President Chiang was asked for his assessment of the Republic of China's situation and for any impression or message that he might wish to convey to the world. He replied: "I am always optimistic. My philosophy is that the more difficulties we encounter, the more we become united. As long as we work hard, we can overcome whatever difficulties we meet along the way. In a speech I gave recently, I emphasized three

A connoisseur of all things Chinese, the President enjoys trying his hand at calligraphy and has great respect for the works of the masters. He is looking at the work of Chang Dai-chien, also famed for his paintings.

Fish cultivation has led to the sport of pond fishing. Like any other fisherman, the President waits for a bite. He learned love of the mountains from his father and often turns to them for rest and solace.

points. The first thing we must do is to establish stability and ensure our survival. After that we can concentrate on development, and finally we will be able to attain victory. Through your magazine, I should like the American people to realize that their genuine, true friends are here in this country. I have every confidence that we can continue our friendship with our American friends, and we shall do everything possible on our part to deserve the confidence of the American people. There is a Chinese expression that no one can wield a knife to cut the ties between two close friends. When I was a young man, I had a great teacher, Mr. Wu Chih-huei. When I complained about all the problems I faced, he responded: 'What are you here for , if not to solve such problems.' "

Although President Chiang was preoccupied with the "U.S. problem" throughout his first year as chief of state, he still found the time and energy to exercise leadership in many other aspects of the nation's life.

He gave special attention to the economy, which showed record growth of 12.8 per cent in 1978. As 1979 gave rise to soaring energy prices and incipient inflation, the chief executive frequently met with his economic ministers and advisers. He stuck to the standard he had followed in his years as

Free China is a land where all religions are free. President Chiang has noted that those who have faith are among the most responsible citizens of the country. Here he looks at fierce temple guardians.

Premier: growth with stability and stability with growth. For the nation, the rewards were great. Through the first half of 1979, fuels derived from oil cost the ultimate consumer only 9 per cent more. The rates for industrial, commercial and household electricity—already among the lowest in the world—were not increased. He said that the lid on prices could be lifted only with damage to the living standard of the people. Inflation was kept under control.

The Ten Major Construction Projects initiated by President Chiang while occuping the premiership were brought to virtual completion in 1979 and blueprints were advanced for the Twelve Construction Projects to carry on infrastructure and other construction benefiting the public. The nine-year education program was made compulsory. Steps were taken to improve the quality as well as the quantity of schooling, and to make sure that each student was prepared to undertake gainful employment upon his graduation from junior high school, senior high school or college. President Chiang was for many years the country's principal youth leader. He retains his deep interest in young people—not only in terms of their education but also with respect to their recreation and physical well-being.

The President's week-ends are customarily spent visiting the countryside to talk with farmers, or going out to see the progress of big construction projects. He also likes to see for himself how the nation's frontline fighters are doing. These expeditions are not holidays. When Chiang Ching-kuo returns to his office on Monday morning, he knows exactly how the people feel about the problems they will be facing that week. He has talked to them—not in his office, not in formal dress and above all, not intimidatingly. He has talked as a friendly uncle interested in how his nephews and nieces are doing and in what they are thinking. He then applies what he learned in day-to-day statecraft.

There is no single problem of the country that does not receive the personal attention of the President. He is a generalist with specialized knowledge of everything that is going on—not because he reads books or listens to briefings so much as because he finds out for himself. Whether he is visiting a beekeeper to learn of advanced methods of encouraging honey production or checking on safety at one of Taiwan's three nuclear power plants, he has more questions than the average specialist can answer.

President Chiang still goes often to the resting place of his late father, President Chiang Kai-shek, at Tzuhu in the peace-

ful rolling hills southwest of Taipei. There he gathers inspiration from the teachings of his parent and mentor. In "Thoughts About My Father at Tzuhu," Chiang Ching-kuo has written: "When I was a youth and Father discovered a wrong or incorrectly written character in letters to him, he was certain to indicate the mistake and send the corrected letters back to me with an admonishment not to repeat my errors. Whatever I said or did, Father was always the same. No sooner had I made a single mistake than he would correct me, paying the closest attention to the most minute detail. I recall that in June of the year before last (1973), Father sent me to Fengshan to preside over graduation ceremonies at the Military Academy. As I was about to leave his room, Father looked at me for a long while and concluded that my hair was not quite in order. He told me to have a haircut before going to the Military Academy. This may seem a small matter, yet it was highly significant."

From the late President Chiang Kai-shek, today's President Chiang Ching-kuo learned the importance of detail. President Chiang Kai-shek once said: "Although I came of a well-to-do family, I was still required in my childhood to help with household work such as washing clothes, sweeping floors and cooking, not occasionally but every single day. My mother required this of me because she wanted to instill in me a spirit of discipline and a true respect for labor. Such training in childhood is invaluable in developing lifelong habits of hard work and in creating good citizens." Chiang Kai-shek impressed diligence and duty upon his elder son, who escaped none of life's menial tasks merely because his father was a great man.

President Chiang Ching-kuo's first year in office was a time of testing, and the new chief executive came through with flying colors. The nation faced problems and difficulties as it entered the second year of the Chiang Ching-kuo administration, but the people shared the high confidence of the man they had chosen to be chief executive.

In electing Chiang Ching-kuo president of the Republic of China, the National Assembly declared: "In view of Mr. Chiang's wisdom and wide experience and considering his loyalty to the nation, his courage in fulfilling his duties, his strong anti-Communist determination, his world prestige and his immense contributions to national construction, the members are confident that he will surely be able to lead the people of the country, military and civilian alike, in overcoming any and all difficulties, carrying out (President Chiang Kai-shek's) will of anti-Communism and mainland recovery more

President Chiang Kai-shek had a great influence on his elder son, President Chiang Ching-kuo. The chief executive returns often to the places he visited with his father. Among them is the lovely meeting of hills and water at Chiaopanshan, Tachi.

No major construction project escapes the personal attention of President Chiang. He went by launch to check on progress of an under-the-harbor tunnel at Hsiaokang in the southern port city of Kaohsiung.

expeditiously and opening up a new vista for our country." The confidence of the Republic of China's electoral college was not misplaced.

In speaking of leadership, President Chiang Kai-shek once said: "In the history of our dynasties, heroes and sages have courageously taken up the responsibility for national salvation in many crises. They have enhanced national spirit, reasserted hereditary moral principles, burnished the truth and reversed wrongful trends of society." The Republic of China was fortunate to have President Chiang Ching-kuo as its leader in another time of crisis and in succession to Dr. Sun Yat-sen, the Founding Father, and President Chiang Kai-shek.

Kueishan (Turtle Mountain) is an islet off Ilan on the east coast. This view is across the vast stretches of the blue Pacific, an ocean which has loomed large in President Chiang's strategic thinking.

# DOCUMENTS
May 1978 to
May 1979

## Inaugural Address

*May 20, 1978*

More than 80 years ago, our National Father, Dr. Sun Yat-sen, contributed his great wisdom, love and courage to the launching of the great undertaking of the nation's and the people's salvation. He led eleven uprisings and was defeated ten times. Eventually the providential and popular revolutionary movement based on the Three Principles of the People succeeded and thereby opened up a new horizon of national revival and established the first free democratic nation in Asia. President Chiang Kai-shek devoted himself to the Revolution and carried on Dr. Sun's unfinished task. Throughout his life he adhered to the belief that: "If the Chinese people are to save their country and themselves, their philosophy must be that of the Three Principles of the People and their revolutionary movement must be that of the National Revolution." From beginning to end, the people of our country have followed the leadership of the Three Principles of the People. Together, we have contributed our thought and our strength. We have given our sweat and blood in the common cause. We have carried out our revolutionary tasks one after another. Today's great task of resisting Communism and achieving national recovery conspicuously carries on the moral and legal line of the National Revolution based on the Three Principles of the People, exalts the national spirit and continues the thorough implementation of revolutionary action.

The National Assembly, acting on the mandate of the people, elected me the sixth President of the Republic of China in accordance with the Constitution. Vice President Shieh Tung-min and I have taken the oath of office and assumed our solemn responsibilities today. We shall always bear the oath in mind: to observe the Constitution, faithfully perform our duties, promote the welfare of the people and safeguard the security of the country. We will in no way betray the people's trust.

In following the consistent course of the National Revolution, we are now facing a crucial test of a new era in a new situation.

The fierce conflict confronting us will decide our fate: glory or humiliation, freedom or slavery. So we look toward the struggle with strengthened determination and ever greater certainty of our success. We must at the same time recognize clearly that:

— This is not an era of individualism, but a time in which everyone is called upon to contribute his wisdom and ability in return for the promise of sharing the fruits of success.

— Magnificent deeds of revolution for national salvation do not make up a beautiful arch covered with flowers. Instead, they constitute a great wall built with sweat and blood.

— Morality and truth should be placed above everything else, and public interest should come before private interest. We should set a goal for our common endeavors and gear our concepts and our action to our sense of responsibility for the country and the nation and the people, with whom we are joined by ties of blood.

The objective of our present common undertaking to recover and reconstruct our country is the increasing of our national strength, improvement of the livelihood of our people, expansion of the functions of constitutional rule and the assurance of honest and competent government to implement the Three Principles of the People and recover the mainland. To express this more explicitly, we may say:

First, we must vigorously augment our national strength, which is basic to national recovery and reconstruction. We currently need not only to root our economic and national defense construction deeply, but also to work hard for political, social and cultural advancement. We must make use of every minute, value every unit of our material power, and pool the wisdom and talent of all so that we can accentuate both our visible national defense combat capability and our invisible political, social and cultural vitality, and combine these into a powerful, compact and undivided force.

Second, we must continue to improve the livelihood of the people. Our economic development in this bastion of national recovery has led to the augmentation of national income, narrowed the gap between rich and poor and increased job opportunities. These are concrete and glorious results of implementing the Principle of the People's Livelihood and also an expression of the vigorous creative spirit of our people and of their strenuous ventures and common struggle. Economic development must not only raise the living standard of the people but must also increase our strength for national recovery and reconstruction. This means that at this juncture we should use our resources according to plan, sustain economic growth, ensure the stability of commodity prices and assure a better life for the people, thereby providing a balance among stability, justice and freedom. We thus can continuously push forward our economic development and increase the people's economic blessing despite international economic competition and buffeting.

In his inaugural address, President Chiang Ching-kuo said the nation was facing a crucial test of new era in a new situation. He pledged "every sacrifice" to assure the final victory

Third, we must work hard to enlarge the scope of constitutional rule. The Chinese government must travel the path of democracy and freedom, and constitutional government is fundamental in the implementation of democracy and freedom. Chinese civilians and soldiers created our glorious constitutional government with their sacrifices, sweat and blood. We can never permit this fundamental achievement to be besmirched or jeopardized. To the contrary, we must enlarge political participation, safeguard freedom and human rights and assure that democracy and freedom are based on the will of all the people and can be advanced in accordance with moral rationality, dignity of the law, common harmony and sincere solidarity.

Fourth, we must ensure all-around honesty and efficiency in government. Everyone has the right and responsibility for participation in national affairs. To make sure that everyone contributes his wisdom, ability, and virtue to the nation and society, we must cultivate and promote talented people in every possible way and for every purpose that accords with the principles of justice. Additionally, we must strengthen social education so as to improve social customs and thus make use of political renovation to assure a high level of constructive political morale. This will complement honesty with efficiency and assure the establishment of a sincere, moral and open society and a truly democratic government.

These actions and constructions are our primary steps in carrying out the Three Principles of the People. Our construction here in the bastion of national recovery has proved that only the Three Principles of the People can save the country and ensure our self-salvation. This also provides a sharp contrast with the performance of the Chinese Communist regime on the mainland — a contrast between benevolence and violence, between happiness and agony, between brightness and darkness and between total right and total wrong.

Consequently, we are increasingly concerned about our compatriots struggling in the crucible of Communist tyranny. We must concentrate our will and muster our strength so as to hasten our actions to recover the mainland and set the people free.

We can say positively and clearly that the Republic of China will never change its determination to remain in the democratic camp and oppose Communism. We shall never change our position of not negotiating or compromising with the Communist enemy. Our fundamental policy and attitude in international politics is to strengthen friendly and moral relations with free nations and fulfill all of our obligations and responsibilities under the preconditions of anti-Communism and national recovery. Strengthening of our relationship with the United States is our consistent policy and principle because of our conviction:

— That anything which benefits China will also benefit the United States and that anything which harms China will also harm the United States. If the two countries stick together, both will benefit; if they are separated, both will suffer.

— That any thought of regarding the Chinese Communists as a "balancing force" or as a party to the "strategy of balance of power," or any illusion that the "building of bridges" and "negotiation" would curtail Chinese Communist expansionism, will confront the free nations with the dilemma of "battling a tiger at the front door" while "letting a wolf in through the back door" — a dilemma in which attack will come from both the front and the rear.

We are confident that the free nations will consider their long-term interests and make long-range plans to control aggression with strength and provide the moral courage to assure true world peace, stability and prosperity.

Three years has elapsed since President Chiang Kai-shek passed away. As a result of the guidance of our fundamental national policy, the able leadership of President Yen Chia-kan and the sincerity of the people, at home and abroad, in pursuing solidarity and self-reliance, we have surmounted the adverse tides of these last three years by helping each other overcome the difficulties of the times. This demonstrates that so long as we can unite and then unite more strongly, struggle and then struggle more strongly, we can withstand the buffeting of any storm or tide and pass any kind of test.

Since I placed myself in the service of the government, I have

consistently established the goal and accepted the duty of devoting myself to the furtherance of national righteousness, the fulfillment of revolutionary responsibility and the assurance of national honor and prestige. With the trust and under the supervision of all the people of the country, I shall from now on try my best and most sincerely and call on all my wisdom and ability to face the challenge of reality with fortitude and determination in company with all my compatriots of the nation. I shall make careful plans and seek judicious judgments to attain the goals of national construction. I shall make every sacrifice to demonstrate my loyalty and give myself to the service of winning the final victory for national recovery and reconstruction together with all the people of the country.

The presidential oath pledges the chief executive to observe the Constitution, promote the welfare of the people and safeguard the security of the state in the faithful performance of his duties.

# Dialogue with David Reed, Editor of Reader's Digest

*May 30, 1978*

*Q. Mr. President, the Republic of China has had more hard knocks than most nations — loss of the mainland, compelled to withdraw from the United Nations, political isolation. Yet the country thrives. How has this been possible?*

A. We have developed despite hardships because we have never abandoned our political objective, that is, to overthrow the mainland's Communist regime and build a united, democratic China. Fortunately we have great internal unity. The people and the government have always stood together and worked together. Since the government moved to Taiwan, we have developed the economy from zero to what it is today, and this has enabled us to be politically secure. Moreover, that security is bolstered by a strong defense: more than half of our government budget goes for defense.

*Q. On the mainland, you were stronger than the Communists, militarily, financially and in other respects. How, then, did they become the victors?*

A. It is a question I'm frequently asked. From the time the Republic of China was established in 1911 until 1949 and especially during the war against Japan, we didn't have time to pay proper attention to internal affairs. By infiltration, by intangible force, they usurped the mainland and forced us to leave.

It was a lesson we didn't forget: that we could not allow any Communist activity in our army, our economy, our schools, or anywhere else in our society. When we came here in 1949, there were Communist guerrilla bases in the suburbs of Taipei. There were Communist organizations in the railroad administration, and secret organizations in our army and factories. Their activities were coordinated by the Communist organization on the mainland. It took us three years, but we got rid of them.

*Q. Some say that infiltration by Communist agents to stir up trouble is still the real threat facing the Republic of China. Do you share that concern?*

A. We are paying a great deal of attention to this problem. Last year, the Communists established a committee responsible for infiltrating Taiwan. We have discovered several instances of espionage. But we have the ability to overcome this problem.

*Q. There are others who argue that the Republic's biggest threat is neither invasion nor infiltration, but slow economic strangulation. Are you having economic difficulties because of your increasing political isolation?*

A. Not having diplomatic relations with other countries does affect us economically, of course. Nevertheless, our trade volume last year was close to US$18 billion. We now have trade relations with more than 120 countries and territories. And we want to continue to expand our trade with others—as long as they are not Communist countries.

*Q. President Carter recently sent a message to Hua Kuo-feng saying that the United States is "committed to normalization of relations with the People's Republic of China on the basis of the Shanghai Communique"—which was made in February, 1972 in which the U.S. and the Communist regime agreed that the normalization of relations between the two countries is not only in the interest of the Chinese and American people but also contributes to the relaxation of tension in Asia and the world. Can the Republic of China continue to prosper, indeed survive, if this happens?*

A. The Republic of China has never considered the so-called Shanghai Communique—signed by Chou En-lai and the ousted Nixon administration—a valid legal document. As to the question of our survival, I have always said that our interests and those of American cannot be divided. If we stick together, both will benefit. If we go separate ways, both will suffer. In any case, the Republic of China will persist.

*Q. It has been proposed that the United States adopt the "Japanese formula" vis-a-vis the Republic of China—not have diplomatic relations, but still have strong trade relations. What is your reaction?*

A. We cannot even entertain the idea. The two cases are quite different. The Republic of China and the United States have had formal and friendly relations for years. We have fought side by side against the Japanese aggressors. China and America have a Mutual Defense Treaty, ratified by the United States Senate. This treaty has legal status.

*Q. When will your forces return to the mainland?*

A. It is difficult to say just when it will take place, but we will return, at the suitable time. As I see it, there are two ways the Communist regime may go. One is by the uprising of the people on the mainland. The second way is by internal division within the regime itself. We must grasp these opportunities, and also create opportunities.

*Q. Do you think Hua Kuo-feng will promote a more humane form of Communism than did Mao Tse-tung?*

A. Impossible. The regime's oppression of the mainland Chinese will inevitably become more and more severe, because without it, the people would revolt immediately. Yet the more you oppress them, the more pressure you put on people to rise in revolt.

*Q. Is it possible, within the foreseeable future, that your government will try to reduce tensions or work out some sort of a peaceful solution with the mainland regime?*

A. That is totally impossible. Negotiating with the Communists is tantamount to suicide. What free-

President Chiang has been a longtime lover of the countryside both in Taiwan and on the mainland. He has visited most scenic locales on the island. The Chinese think sightseeing should start at home. Many suspension bridges like this grace Taiwan.

world country has ever successfully done so? Negotiations are a means the Communists use to defeat their enemies. We can't forget this because when we were on the mainland we tried some negotiation with the Communists. The more we negotiated, the more setbacks we suffered. Never, even under the difficult circumstances, will we negotiate with them again. This is the most fundamental policy of the Republic of China.

*Q. Recently the Carter administration reported that while what it calls human rights violations in the Republic of China have diminished such violations "continue to occur." Is the report accurate?*

A. The fundamental difference between the Republic of China and the mainland's Communist regime is that we do protect human rights. Respect for human rights is a moral principle this government fully supports, an important aspect of our anti-Communist struggle. But if a person is working for the Communists, against our anti-Communist policy of safeguarding human rights and people's freedom —then of course that is quite a different story.

*Q. Earlier we talked about the remarkable economic progress the Republic of China has been making. What developments do you see in this area in the years to come?*

A. We must control the budget and not go into the red. This is an absolute. The government also must control market prices in order to avoid inflation and have continued economic stability. There may be other nations that are developing even more rapidly, but not with the

degree of stability we have.

By the end of next year, most of the 10 major construction projects now under way will have been essentially completed. Then we will start another 12. At the same time, it is important that we use our land and water effectively, and mechanize our agriculture. We also want to change our labor-intensive industries to more sophisticated, technologically advanced ones. This way we can improve the quality of our exports to better compete with other countries. This will gradually improve the standard of living, helping our people to live better lives; this year better than the last, and next year better than this.

*Q. Why did you decide to run for President instead of remaining Premier?*

A. I am a member of the Kuomintang, the ruling party. Since the party nominated me for the office of the presidency, I agreed to run.

*Q. Some people interpreted the selection of Shieh Tung-min as Vice-President as a move to meet the political aspirations of those of your citizens born in Taiwan. Will more Taiwanese assume high posts?*

A. When I nominated Mr. Shieh Tung-min as my running mate, I never thought about where he comes from. I knew only that he is Chinese. As a matter of fact, all the people in Taiwan are Chinese. As Vice President Shieh himself has said, we all came to Taiwan from the mainland.

The only difference is some came first, others came later.

# Dialogue with Kim Tai Hong, Commentator of the Korean Broadcasting System

*August 22, 1978*

*Q. First of all I congratulate you on Your Excellency's assumption of the Presidency of the Republic of China and thank you for your kindness for granting me this interview. Would you tell me what is your basic policy after taking up the presidency?*

A. Thank you for your congratulations, Mr. Kim. Let me explain the fundamental policy of the Republic of China in four points:

1. We will never change the national system stipulated in the Constitution of the Republic of China.

2. We will never abandon our goal of opposing Communism for national recovery.

3. We will always stand on the side of the democratic camp and will never join up with any Communist regime or bloc.

4. We will never make peace with the bogus Chinese Communist regime that occupies the Chinese mainland. We will fight to the finish to attain our goal of national reunification.

*Q. Your Excellency, what is your policy for national development and national recovery? What is the future goal of the country?*

A. Our national development requires a long-range program, so we have formulated long-range goals. On the one hand, we will enable the people in Taiwan, Penghu, Kinmen and Matsu to lead a life of freedom and prosperity, and on the other hand we will tell our compatriots on the mainland that they can get rid of Communist rule only by pursuing the free way of life. We are using this political call to awaken our mainland compatriots to resist the Communist regime. We also have the ultimate goal of carrying out Dr. Sun Yat-sen's Three Principles of the People, unifying China and establishing a free, equitable and strong Republic of China.

*Q. What is Your Excellency's assessment and view with regard to the current changes in the Chinese Communist regime, including Hua Kuo-feng's acceding to power and the adoption of a pragmatic line?*

A. At the moment, the Chinese Communists face immense domestic problems, politically, economically and militarily. To maintain their rule, they have to accept an internal compromise, but this compromise is temporary, not permanent. Eventually, serious conflict will erupt within the regime. They are now clamoring for "modernization," but modernization must be based on freedom. Without freedom, there will be no modernization. There can be none under despotic and tyrannical rule. They are using the "modernization" slogan to deceive and placate the people on the mainland.

*Q. Do you think there is a really substantive conflict between Moscow and Peking? If so, what is Your Excellency's position. If not, what is your explanation?*

A. It is basically wrong to assume that the conflict between Moscow and Peiping is one between two countries and two peoples. This is really a struggle for leadership between two Communist parties. There is no question of nation and people, but a rivalry for leadership of the international Communist movement. Because the struggle for leadership is decisive to their survival, the Chinese Communists will carry it on to the end. This life-or-death struggle shows that their internal schism is irreparable.

*Q. What is your view of U.S. withdrawal of its ground forces from Korea? Do you think this move will affect the security of Korea and the stability of the whole of Northeast Asia?*

A. The security of Korea is related not only to the security of Asia but also to that of all the world. The United States should not reduce its military presence in Korea. On the contrary, it should increase its military strength to prevent the southward advance of the Communist forces.

*Q. The international political structure has undergone rapid change. What is your view of the future development of world order?*

A. It is true the world is changing rapidly. We may also say it is changing constantly. But basically we must understand that no matter how it changes, the situation is still a struggle between Communism and anti-Communism, between slavery and anti-slavery and between tyranny and freedom.

Kim Tai Hong of the Korean Broadcasting System received President Chiang's

We Chinese, and I think all Orientals, are convinced that justice will prevail. No matter how the world may change, we believe freedom will prevail over violence and the free world will defeat the Communist world.

*Q. The economic development of your country and my country have won worldwide acclaim. What are the main elements of these developments?*

A. The rapid and successful economic development of the Republic

message for people of the Republic of Korea on the occasion of the 30th anniversary of the ROC's friendly northern neighbor.

Beaches are popular with the people during the long hot Taiwan summer. This is Fulung on the northern coast, which is easily reached from Taipei by special train. A new northeast coastal highway has opened additional stretches of beach in this same general area.

of Korea in the last few years is a result of first, the strong leadership of President Park Chung Hee, second, the meticulous long-range planning, and third, the hard work of the Korean people and their support of the government. So I believe your economic success is also your political success.

*Q. How is your view of President Park's able leadership in endlessly seeking economic growth and national security?*

A. The government and people of the Republic of China were happy to see President Park's election and re-election. We have been gratified at President Park's outstanding contributions not only to the national development of the Republic of Korea but also to the security and peace of Asia. I am convinced that under President Park's continuing leadership, the Republic of Korea will become stronger and more stable. He deserves my special congratulations.

*Q. What is your view of the interrelationship among political stability, economic development and political leadership?*

A.Economy and politics are indivisible. The goal of economic development is to fulfill the political objective; politics is the motive power for economic development. We are undertaking well-planned economic development with a prescribed goal. We may also say this is a program for the country and the people. So we believe there are four important elements in national development: economy, politics, education and national defense. A country can become strong only after these four elements are forged

into one.

*Q. As the Republics of China and Korea have common interests and fortune, would you tell me how the two nations should strengthen their cooperation to ensure their mutual interest?*

A. The Republic of Korea and the Republic of China have a common ground in almost everything, but especially in thought, philosophy and social concept. These have been the cornerstones of our close cooperation in the past. As we have laid a firm foundation for cooperation, I am convinced that despite today's changing world situation and many mutual problems, our two countries will be able to further cooperation and strengthen friendly relations with the passing of each day.

*Q. This year is the 30th anniversary of the founding of the Republic of Korea. Do you have any congratulatory message to the people of Korea?*

A. In 30 years of hard struggle, the Republic of Korea has had times of success and times of adversity. In both success and adversity, Korea can be proud of itself. The Republic of Korea has never faltered in its struggle for independence, unification and freedom. The hard struggle of these 30 years has convinced the government and people of the Republic of Korea that victory is inevitable. I am sure that under President Park's able leadership the people of the Republic of Korea will turn back Communist aggression and ultimately attain their goal of national unification.

# National Day Congratulatory Message

*October 10, 1978*

The Double Tenth National Day of the Republic of China is the supremely glorious and festive day of the people of the entire country. This day symbolizes page after page of our historical interweaving of triumph and difficulty. It also reflects the Chinese people's noble character of forbearance, fortitude and total rectitude.

Sixty-seven years ago today, our National Father, who was motivated by his great benevolence, wisdom and courage, rallied uncounted numbers of revolutionaries to save the nation and the people. Enduring immense suffering and sacrifice, they established the first democratic republic in Asia. Even so, internal problems and external aggression were never overcome, and the country never knew a single day of peace. President Chiang Kai-shek then embarked upon his great career of heroic deeds. He led the National Revolution with tremendous and invincible courage and his great spirit of sacrifice. He carried out the monumental tasks of the Northward Expedition, the repulsing of

Japanese aggression and the implementation of constitutional government. In the struggle against Communism, he established this powerful bastion for national recovery and revival. These are facts which amply attest that Chinese sons and daughters are aware of their responsibility to nation and people, and which also attest to their courage in accepting the duty of rescuing the world from the brink of destruction. These same facts serve to prove that benevolence is invincible and that justice always triumphs. So we can say that the Double Tenth National Day has many meanings. This is a festival to be celebrated and at the same time a revelation of our responsibility. It goads us to action and inspires us to succeed. Because this National Day is celebrated as the 50th anniversary of victory in the Northward Expedition and national reunification, our perceptions are deeper and clearer than ever before.

Today, our enemies, the Chinese Communists, are yet to be destroyed and the undertow of appeasement still persists in the world. So our nation and people are faced with harder and sterner tests. The huge responsibility of meeting these challenges rests squarely on the shoulders of each Chinese son and daughter at home or abroad who upholds freedom and democracy and opposes Communism and slavery. All the conscientious and righteous offspring of Chinese ancestors are bound to follow in the footsteps of our courageous and unconquerable forefathers and national martyrs and to undertake any sacrifice in our sacred cause by taking up the responsibility for struggle against Communism and

One of the highlights of the Double Tenth National Day is the setting off of fireworks over the river just west of the gaily decorated Presidential Building in downtown Taipei. President and people meet here.

for national recovery.

The overall goal of the National Revolution in the present stage is to carry out the Three Principles of the People and recover the Chinese mainland. This will extend the structure and accomplishments of our benevolent government and the progress made in our bastion of national recovery to every corner of the mainland, enabling all of our compatriots to enjoy freedom, democracy, peace and happiness with us and to rearm themselves with the spiritual strength of Chinese culture. We are convinced that we shall succeed by rallying ourselves to support this overall objective,

unifying our will, strengthening our convictions and demonstrating the sincerity and solidarity of our struggle.

We swear to make the national flag of blue sky and white sun shine always with brilliance on the Double Tenth National Day and to assure the strength and happiness of coming generations of the Chinese people. Let us pray together for national prosperity. Let us raise these cheers, loudly and in unison:

Long live the Three Principles of the People!

Long live the Republic of China!

# Remarks at
# the Military
# Parade

*October 10, 1978*

My Dear Fellow Countrymen and Honorable Guests:

The magnificent ranks of the grand military parade held on this Double Tenth National Day included the following:

— Officers and men of the Army, Navy, Air Force, Combined Service and Garrison forces.

— Fighters from the frontlines of Kinmen and Matsu.

— Reservists from our bastion of national recovery.

— Outstanding representatives of people who are serving the nation on various fronts.

In this parade, I have seen the perfect cadence of the march, the high spirits and the magnificent military posture. This has conclusively shown that the armed forces of the Republic of China are superbly trained and that their morale is extraordinarily high. The various weapons paraded past the reviewing stand, although representing only a very small fraction of the total, attested to the profound potential of our armed forces in producing weapons and to their high skill in using them. In particular, this parade manifested the combat spirit of our armed forces of both the battle-front and the production front deriving from their tight organization, close cooperation, common will and concentrated strength. This revolutionary spirit coupled with these modern weapons has given rise to forces that will surely triumph in any battle or carry out any attack. I am convinced that they will succeed in their sacred, honorable and historic task of defending this bastion of national revival and recovering the mainland.

I want to express my gratification and extend my best wishes to all the officers and men who have taken part in the parade.

Viewing this military parade, our compatriots at home and abroad can clearly see that our country is moving ahead, that we have made progress in social development and that the combat capability of our armed forces is increasing. These facts are incontrovertible evidence of the promising future of our country and people.

Fellow countrymen: Although we are now faced with a difficult situation, as long as we can unite totally and sincerely, exert ourselves, carry out President Chiang Kai-shek's teachings, accumulate our gains little by little and move forward step by step, we can overcome the difficulties, defeat the enemy, open up a new vista, wipe out the Chinese Communists, recover our territory, set free our compatriots on the mainland and win the final victory that has always belonged to us!

Let us send up these resounding cheers:

Long live our victory in the battle against Communism and for national recovery!

Long live the Three Principles of the People!

Long live the Republic of China!

Military leaders of the Republic join President Chiang in reviewing the Double Tenth military parade from in front of the Presidential Building in Taipei. The chief executive called for defense preparedness.

# Dialogue with Renzo Trionfera, International Political Correspondent of Il Giornale Nuovo of Milan, Italy

*October 10, 1978*

*Q. Mr. President, it is evident that the diplomatic initiatives launched by Communist China in the international field are aimed at asserting its presence among the THIRD WORLD countries and in the area of the so-called "non-aligned" nations but also in the area of the countries openly leaning toward the West.*

*Besides the evident intention of strengthening its relationship with the countries in which there are "currents" that dissent or oppose the U.S.S.R., do you think, Mr. President, that such a political offensive is aiming at further isolating your country from the West and widening the political gap between the ROC and the free world?*

*A.* This question may be answered in two aspects. Internally, the Communist regime faces many problems, including power struggle among Communist leaders and agricultural, educational and economic failures. Consequently, the people on the Chinese mainland are leading increasingly miserable lives and simmering with anger. As a result of these failures, the Communist regime actively launched international offensives to divert the people's attention. Externally, the Communist regime caused trouble for the Soviet Union all over the world and especially in Europe to alleviate the Russians' frontal pressures.

The Chinese Communist intrigues to isolate the Republic of China will never succeed. This is made evident by the fact that the Republic of China has improved its substantial cultural, economic and social relations with all countries of the free world.

More than 140 countries and areas have commercial relations with us. The Republic of China's two-way trade reached US$17.6 billion in 1977, and the 1978 volume is expected to surpass US$23 billion. These figures exceed the trade of the Communist regime with a population of 800 million.

The Republic of China is ranked 22nd among the trading nations of the world.

*Q. Although Taiwan is no more represented at the U.N. and maintains diplomatic relations only with the USA—among the great industrial and military powers—, it is very successfully developing its commercial and cultural ties not only with America and the countries of Asia but also with Europe.*

*Do you think, Mr. President, you will be in a position to plan and carry out a new diplomatic action so that your free country could regain the place it deserves among the international agencies and institutions and in the diplomatic relations with the rest of the free world?*

A. The Republic of China is willing to establish relations with any freedom-loving and democratic country in the world.

Fundamentally, the relations between countries are based on common interest. The Republic of China has been a constructive member of the international community.

I believe that friendly and reciprocal relations will be developed between my country and many other democratic countries.

*Q. Do you consider, Mr. President, as a possibility in the long run, a stabilization of the Asian fluctuating situation which could bring about a "modus vivendi" of NON AGGRESSION between the two Chinas?*

A. We have repeatedly reminded the free world that Asian turmoil is the result of Chinese Communist aggression and expansion. While the Chinese Communists usurp the Chinese mainland, Asia will never have peace.

The Korean war and Vietnam war were masterminded and backed by the Communist regime from behind the scenes. So as long as the Chinese Communist regime exists, there can be no lasting Asian peace and stability.

We must point out that so-called "two Chinas" and "non-aggression" pledges are the wishful thinking of those who lack a full understanding of the China issue. The Chinese Communists are an insurgent group in our territory and we don't recognize its legal status.

The Republic of China's fundamental policy of not talking to or compromising with this insurgent group will never be changed.

*Q. There have been recently persistent rumors about the reduction of foreign aid (particularly military aid) from Washington to your country. In case of an aggression, is Taiwan in a position to assure its own defense so as to preserve its independence and territorial integrity?*

*Do you think your country could acquire an important role in the defense of the non-Communist countries in the Far East?*

A. All of our civilian and military compatriots are united and prepared and confident to repulse any invasion by the Communist Chinese armed forces. However, we need moral, spiritual and logistical support from free and friendly countries of the world.

Korea, Japan and Taiwan form

Another of Taiwan's scenic spectaculars is the Penglai falls in Chiayi County of the central western area. President Chiang is not only an ardent sightseer himself but has been active in supporting road and rail projects to open up mountainous and once inaccessible Taiwan to home tourism and to visitors coming from faraway lands.

a vital chain of defense. Our powerful 500,000 standing armed forces and 2,200,000 reservists make up the indispensable bulwark of peace and stability in the area.

*Q. There have been delicate and difficult moments between Taipei and Washington in the past which were brought about by the American attitude and desire to arrive at a normalization of relationship with Communist China. Do you think these difficulties have been overcome now? What is the actual situation of your relations with Washington as things are today?*

A. For the time being, the relations between the Republic of China and the United States are normal. The friendship of the Congress and the state legislatures of the United States reflect the wish of the majority of American people.

We believe the U.S. government will not ignore these facts. Because of the lengthy relationship between our two countries, any change in the tie between the Republic of China and the United States would have a substantial impact on all Asia. The U.S. government has to be careful.

*Q. Mr. President, your country is still living in a state of emergency even if the external aspects of this situation are not easily noticeable. In which way is the domestic situation of Taiwan (in its various aspects) conditioned (or influenced) by this state of emergency?*

*Mr. President, what are the possibilities of a further normalization and larger democratization that you can envision for the future of the ROC?*

A. The Republic of China is in the period of Communist rebellion. The Communist regime across the Taiwan straits will never give up its ambition to invade and occupy Taiwan. In the face of a formidable foe, we cannot neglect our national defense. We must make ourselves stronger.

The Chinese Communists have set up a "Taiwan office" under the "state council" to plot against us. So we must be vigilant against their conspiracies of infiltration, division, sabotage and subversion. This is a situation differing from that faced by any other country.

Despite this situation, we never lose a day in our efforts to implement constitutional democracy. Elections for representatives and local government officials in the Taiwan district have been held regularly for a long time. The people have formed the habit of exercising their democratic civil rights.

Elections for central government representatives will be held in Taiwan, Penghu, Kinmen and Matsu at the end of this year. Meanwhile, our courts have consistently honored to the letter the principle of independent trials.

The basic rights of the people are protected in accordance with the Constitution.

We are moving in the direction established for us by the late President Chiang Kai-shek. This is "to realize the Three Principles of the People and to remain in the democratic camp." We shall continue to move in this direction.

# Remarks on the 33rd Anniversary of the Restoration of Taiwan

*October 25, 1978*

Today is the 33rd anniversary of the Restoration of Taiwan.

This is a glorious day. The people of Taiwan suffered 50 years of oppression before regaining their freedom 33 years ago. This is also a traumatic day, because Taiwan and Penghu were returned to the jurisdiction of the Republic of China only after the people of the country had fought against the Japanese for 14 years with the loss of uncounted numbers of lives and inestimable quantities of money and materials. This is also an historic day, because in the last 33 years the whole body of the people has united with the government sincerely and strongly in the common effort to create our socie-ty of stability, progress and afflu-ence.

The restoration of Taiwan 33 years ago brought every Chinese into the mainstream of our national culture and history. We are linked to one another by blood and are responsible to each other in conse-quence of our sincerity. Everyone in this bastion of national recovery has a sense of the historic relation-ship of Taiwan and the mainland and strong feelings of national responsibility. This burning historic sensibility and powerful sense of national responsibility have been translated into action to accelerate development of our bastion and preparations for national recovery.

Since the Restoration of Taiwan, we have suffered the buffeting of adverse international political tides and economic upheavals. But we have never been worried or apprehensive. We have followed the course of our principles. We have striven to fulfill our national responsibility with one will and one heart, and have carried out political, economic, social and cultural development step by step. We have regarded the great devotion shown by our mainland compatriots in recovering Taiwan 33 years ago as our spiritual lodestar for the national recovery of today. We have built a psychological Great Wall and persisted in our confident waging of the struggle against Communism with total sincerity and the fortitude essential to success.

As the late President Chiang Kai-shek told us, we have in this bastion of Taiwan the perseverance of the whole body of the people, the determined support of loyal overseas Chinese throughout the world and the expectations and longing of the multitudes of compatriots on the mainland. The starting point of carrying out our national responsibility and consummating our historic task of national revival lies in recovering the mainland in the same spirit that we restored Taiwan.

I wish all of you happiness, well-being and peace.

Lions dance and dragons prance on festive occasions. The gate is that of the Grand Hotel on Taipei's northside. The occasion was Taiwan Restoration Day, marking return of the island to China by Japan on October 25 of 1945.

# Thinking of Father

*October 31, 1978*

## I

A young artist, Lin Tsung-hui, spent six months in the mountains at Hualien looking for a supernally white slab of marble, then sculpted the piece into a three-foot full-length figure of my father. Depicting Father standing in long gown and carrying his walking stick, the statue solemnly expresses Father's tranquillity and benignity. I respectfully accepted the sincere gift from the sculptor and placed the statue on a stand in front of the desk in my office.

Father passed away more than three years ago, and I can no longer hear his strict instructions or bask in his kindness and benevolence. But when I am so engrossed in my work that I can hardly take even a brief moment of respite, I instinc-tively raise my head and look into the eyes of Father's statue. Suddenly I can hear Father's voice advising me to rally my spirits with an interlude of calm and relaxation. Immediately, I am able to brace up again and feel the resurgence of life. When I am pondering a problem and find my mind confused, the brilliant light from the eyes of Father's statue penetrates my heart and opens up the clogged channels of thought. The problem is resolved. In his lifetime, he was my leader, my kindly father and my stern teacher. I am still under the influence of his love.

## II

For all his lifetime, Father's words and deeds were deeply influenced by Confucius, Mencius and Dr. Sun Yat-sen. He often said that the most important teaching of Confucius and Mencius was "to apply one's learning in one's work." Father always practiced this philosophy — in his behavior and morals and his political and spiritual life. We know that he was a Confucian who loved the people and cherished all things. From the time he began to follow Dr. Sun Yat-sen in waging the Revolution, he respected the National Father as his own father and teacher. He gave a lifetime's adherence to Dr. Sun's teachings and vowed that he would never rest until these had been carried out. We also know that he cared only for the Three Principles of the People and was unconcerned about his own life or death. He never ceased trying to implement the Three Principles and carry out the National Revolution.

The exploits and moral accomplishments of his life embodied the thought and practice of Confucius, Mencius and Dr. Sun Yat-sen and marked the fruition of his lifelong endeavors. This was also the expression of an altruism that sought the salvation of the nation and the world. Dr. John Wu said: "President Chiang Kai-shek's altruism may be thought of as a philosophy of the Cross. In devoting himself to the Revolution for our country and people, he carried the Cross for more than 60 years. Yet he never complained or felt he was overburdened. Rather, he was always youthful in outlook and vigorous in spirit." In fact, when I stand raptly in front of Father's statue, I can clearly see Father's great character and integrity in "carrying the revolutionary cross" and his upright moral stature rising as erectly as a giant pillar supporting the sky.

### III

Once I read an article by Dr. W. G. Goddard of Australia about Father. He quoted an English historian, Edward Gibbon, as saying in *The History of the Decline and Fall of the Roman Empire* that "No biography of a great man should be attempted till at least a century after his death!" Dr. Goddard concluded: "Such a man is Chiang Kai-shek." He said that Father was a great man in our times but that he would be greater still in the eyes of future historians. As a forerunner in thought, the prime-mover of national construction and the prophet of the anti-Communist movement, Father was a great man in his time and a decisive force in the modern historical development of the country and the people. To write the biography of such a great man requires a vision of the future from the world viewpoint of

history as well as judgments based on the present. Up to now, many historians, men of letters and artists have written biographies and poems and have created paintings and statues to perpetuate the greatness of this man. These works have contributed to history and are of great value. More than 10,000 persons from at home and abroad are traveling to Tzuhu each month to pay homage to Father. The Chiang descendants are deeply moved by and appreciative of these expressions of kindness. We can readily perceive that as time passes, the people at home and abroad are increasing their outpouring of respect for this man of the ages. The light and heat radiated from Father have been transformed into the great love of the people. The light becomes brighter with the lengthening of history. People know Father will be even greater in the future than he is now.

### IV

On the eve of Father's 92nd birthday, I read with respect the pages of his diary written in 1923 when he was 37 years old. In some pages, he referred to Dr. Sun Yat-sen as "my teacher." He encouraged himself to become one of Dr. Sun's disciples and exhorted others to do likewise, as in this passage:

*As the party and the nation are in danger of falling apart, my teacher serves as a monolith to uphold them. As the people are withering away in an excruciatingly hard life, my teacher comes to their rescue like a precious shower to save withering crops in a terrible drought.*

The President has written movingly of the inspiration he derives from this marble sculpture of his father, President Chiang Kai-shek. The sculptor, Lin Tsung-hui, is seen here in the President's office.

The following are other passages from the diary:

*Today I have composed this motto for myself: Keep your thought unrestrained for free functioning. This can broaden your vision, brighten your heart and bring you the happiness of fulfillment. This is the way of self-cultivation. In approaching practical affairs, you should begin with the essentials, adhere to the key factors, make detailed analysis and always keep the goal in your hearts.*

*I composed this couplet:*

*Life or death is not worthy of concern; praise or denigration should always be ignored. Then I composed another: Distinguish right from wrong; taste all the flavors of life — the bitter together with the sweet.*

*First, watch over yourself when you are alone and your mind will be at peace. Try to rid yourself of all selfish desires but keep intact the divine reason within yourself. Second, let the spirit of reverence be your master and your whole being will be hale and strong. Be alert to the* perils and pitfalls of life and take care that your power and strength does not lead you into aggressiveness. Third, seek to cultivate humane love and others will be eager to associate with you. Love all people as your brothers and cherish all things. Let your beneficences extend far and wide. Fourth, if you acquire the habit of diligence, it will keep your mind clear. Exert all your energy and use all your power of thought. Learn the hard way and live strenuously.

Life's successes and failures are not predictable. All we can do is follow the dictates of our heart and mind. If our mind tells us a certain thing can be done and predicts there is a better than 50 per cent chance of success, we should go ahead without further vacillation.

In anything we may do, we should not be discouraged and deterred by unnecessary doubts. If we can move ahead steadfastly and courageously, people will yield to our determination and will not dare to obstruct us. They may even come to respect us.

If we want to keep ourselves unperturbed by prosperity or adversity, security or danger, the only way is to keep the mind free of inordinate desire and selfish ambition, and to be composed and detached.

A man who shoulders great responsibility must be supremely tolerant, detached and magnanimous, and not overemphasize the trivial.

To fulfill a great career requires, first of all, the rallying of our spirit. We should ask ourselves whether what we are doing conforms to the principle of justice. We should be unconcerned about failure or success. Life or death, triumph or tragedy, should not matter to us.

These few passages are sufficient to help us see Father's great mindedness and inspiring character as a young man. In his diary, Father summarized these thoughts in four sentences:

—Let your mind be free and untrammeled.

—Let your words be quiet and serene.

—Let your heart be at peace and your vital energy be nurtured.

—Let your spirit be recollected and your complexion be friendly and kind.

This is the sum total of the way of self-cultivation. I have inscribed these sentences on a scroll and hung it on the wall. I read them every day and make them my guideline. As I stand attentively in front of the statue and relive the times of receiving lessons and love from Father, I feel that my gratitude to him is boundless. The goal of my present endeavors is to carry on Father's work of serving the people and sacrificing for the country. So I must regard his thoughts as my thoughts and his mind as my mind.

As I am thinking deeply of Father, my eagerness to sacrifice myself for the country grows in intensity as time passes. This has led me to write this article.

# Address to the Fifth Journalists' Conference

*November 8, 1978*

This conference is held in the hope that journalists will share their thought and wisdom with us, promote the solidarity of the people, further the spirit of democracy and the rule of law, and expedite the attainment of our national goal as they carry out the functions of the mass communications enterprises.

I recall that the Founding Father of the Republic said: "Dissemination of information constitutes 90 per cent of our efforts to assure the quick success of our Revolution." In other words, an invincible revolutionary force can be generated only by publicizing the greatness of the Revolution's meaning, consolidating the psychological preparations of society and strengthening the spiritual armament of the people. Looking back on the more than 80 years since the establishment of our ruling party — from our Founding Father's assumption of national revolutionary leadership to revive China and establish the Republic down to President Chiang Kai-shek's inheritance of the Founding Father's endeavors to eliminate the warlords, resist the aggression of powerful neighbors, implement constitutional rule and construct this bastion of national revival — we can see that our leaders suffered greatly and always sought the freedom and equality of China and the peace and happiness of the people. We may say that their motives shone as brightly as the sun and the moon and that their minds were as broad as the sky and the earth. In these scores of years, the ruling party has undeniably suffered endless misrepresentations, misunderstandings, denigrations and even humiliations. Some of these have been malicious canards, slanders and blows aimed at the party. But I think a contributing factor may be the party's failure to exercise its influence and power of conviction in cultural and press activities intended to plant the principle and objective of the struggle in the hearts of the people of the whole nation.

In the present stage, the sole task of the National Revolution is to complete the great anti-Communist undertaking of national recovery. We may say this is ultimately the most difficult task of the ruling party's revolutionary struggle. The Chinese Communists have occupied the mainland for nearly three decades. Their unprecedented and unwarranted dictatorship has plunged our compatriots on the mainland into the black terror of tyranny and brought catastrophe without parallel to the great cultural tradition of China. This tragedy has not yet ended, but the people of the world seemingly have failed to look squarely at the seriousness of the consequences. Free world appeasers even contribute to the adverse tide by helping the Chinese Communists engage in international united front plots, thus augmenting their evil influence and aggravating the suffering of humankind. This confused world situation in which right is not distinguished from wrong and morality is not separated from immorality has brought more suffering and difficulties in our struggle against Communism and for freedom and justice. We must save the world from such confusion. Our intention is not to endure these sufferings passively but to exert ourselves vigorously and self-reliantly transform our sufferings into victory. This reminds us of something President Chiang Kai-shek had to say while serving as our Founding Father's chief of staff. He said: "It is more difficult to break through a maze of bewilderment than to overwhelm an entrenched position." The "maze of bewilderment" refers to psychological warfare and the "entrenched position" refers to armed combat. Psychological warfare is not restricted by time and space. In this warfare, one must be constantly prepared to take the offensive. In other words, we must have psychological faith in our victory. Our action then will be crowned with success.

We rely on our unswerving faith in succeeding. Years ago, the late President urged us "To be self-reliant with dignity; to be calm in time of adversity." This instruction has generated within us an unflinching fortitude whenever we are subjected to the buffeting of mounting and terrible tides. This also provides us with intensive staying power and is testimony to the effectiveness of our psychological preparation. The situation ahead of us is more treacherous than before. We must be calm and bring into play the power of our faith and establish an impregnable psychological Great Wall. No matter how confused and difficult the world situation may be, we must never be intimidated by sufferings or hardships and must adhere to the principles of anti-Communism and justice. If we are well-prepared to cope with the difficulties, the forces of evil can never prevail. We must unite the people of the nation and encourage one another with counsel of "Do not worry and do not be afraid and act only in accordance with principle." We must partake of joy and sorrow together and demonstrate the revolutionary spirit of justice, sincerity, solidarity and sacrifice in our struggle to meet all challenges, break through all difficulties and win our final and glorious victory.

In this great year of the struggle between the forces of justice and injustice and between freedom and slavery, every journalist should accept the solemn responsibility of attacking evil with the mighty force of his pen. In this moment of national crisis and in the face of the formidable enemy, he should wake the people to the realities of the national goal and to awareness of what should be done and what should not be done in keeping with his patriotism and conscience and by distinguishing justice from self-seeking and good from evil. On

September 1, 1974, I wrote to my journalist friends an open letter under the title "Attack Heresy With the Pen of Justice." This is one passage: "In the course of the Revolution, there is a high tide and a low tide. In the national fortunes, there are successes and failures. In social phenomena, there are bright and dark aspects. To enhance the morale of the people, encourage society and support the national cause, our journalist friends must rely upon their moral courage and wield their mighty pens to publicize the positive and bright side of events. This will rouse the people's conscience and desire to aspire for the better, so that our nation and society can be always fresh and vigorous and can make continuous progress." In my government service of past years, my happiest experiences have been enjoyed while trying to improve the people's lives, strengthen national defenses and improve our society. The people have joined the government in common efforts of national construction in a harmonious, fresh and vigorous atmosphere. This spirit has provided me with the courage and strength to overcome difficulties and provide more service to the country and the people. Today, I am thinking of how to help journalist friends who are working in this confused era rid themselves of uncertainty arising from the current situation and bewilderment growing out of the environment and regain their sound sensibilities. How solemn and important are these responsibilities and this work! So I wish to offer some points of view for reference in your writing and for our mutual encouragement.

First, at this time of ominous change in the world — with the Chinese Communists doing everything they possibly can to destroy us — everyone should regard national salvation as his own responsibility so that we can overcome all adverse tides. I am convinced that under the conditions of today no one should take advantage of the national crisis and engage in illicit activities for private gain in total disregard of the national interest as a whole. I believe all of us need to face reality with fortitude, sobriety and calm. We must swear to be dedicated and courageous. We must be faithful and loyal to our country. We should support the government's anti-Communist policy all the way and fortify the nation's position and power. We should be determined to do so even if we must brave boiling water and furious flames.

Second, to uphold democracy and the constitutional government that enables the people to enjoy a life of liberty and equality, and to teach the people to perceive and experience the true meaning of democratic government so we can march along the right political road and ensure that the opinions of the people are truly respected, I am convinced that in these times no one should undermine our constitutional foundations by spurning public opinion and giving false accounts of the facts. It is essential that everyone respect the law, try to be practical, abide by the rule of law and assume an aboveboard position and a frank and sincere attitude when engaged in legitimate political activities so that we can add luster to our constitutional system.

Third, to seek the continued development and growth of our

national economy under stable conditions and with the goal of improving the lives of the people in the hope of assuring them equitable wealth and happiness, I am convinced that no one should continue to seek private gain at the expense of the people, undermine stability, attempt to fish in troubled waters or put obstacles in the way of national progress. I feel that we urgently require dedication to our work; harmony, mutual assistance and cooperation with others; sharing of our wisdom and demonstration of our allegiance; and the contribution of our talents to the promotion of economic modernization, the enrichment of the people's livelihood and the augmentation of our national strength.

Fourth, to ensure social order and the maintenance of sound customs so that everyone is secure and happy in his life and so that we can stress faith and friendship, I am convinced that there shall be no one who continues to undermine social stability and peace with the intention of plunging the world into disorder by doing evil things and confusing the people with rumors. I think we have utmost need to make certain that everyone abides by the law, fulfills his responsibility and is frugal, diligent, sincere, practical, modest, openminded and patient with others, and develops a noble national morality.

Fifth, to encourage and watch over the government in making administrative renovations and es-

President Chiang shows his respect for journalists by attending their meetings and sending them greetings on special occasions. He gives interviews to many foreign reporters visiting the ROC.

Taipei has grown
from a small city to
a great metropolis
in the 30 years since
the government's
move from the mainland
in 1949. Population
has soared well past
the 2 million mark.
The city is also
the cultural center
of Taiwan Province.

tablishing honest and competent administration providing the people with better and more efficient service, I am convinced that it is important for the people to spur public functionaries and for the government to respect the opinions of the people. No one should continue dampening the morale of government employees by distorting the facts in consequence of personal grievances. I hope the people can give more encouragement and praise to government departments and personnel who are loyal to their duties, courageous in discharging their assignments, clean and patient about their difficulties. I also hope the people will promptly report the derelictions · and corruptions of officials and the bad elements that proffer bribes so that the offenders can be severely punished and we can jointly maintain our political integrity.

Sixth, and especially important at this difficult and perilous time for the nation, we should strengthen the solidarity of the whole body of the people so as to come together in coping with every adverse development. I am convinced that at this moment we urgently require everyone to show an unflinching, dauntless will, determination to ensure success, the sincerity to provide mutual assistance in stormy times and willingness to join hearts and cooperate closely. We shall never allow others to divide and weaken our ranks. In both conceptualization and action, we should give first priority to anti-Communism and national recovery. We should forge millions upon millions of hearts together as one and march forward hand in hand as courageously and unitedly as a

single entity.

I believe deeply that every government has its defects and that everyone is entitled to criticize the government. As long as the government is sincere with the people and the people can trust the government, defects and criticisms are merely steps in the process of renovation and progress. I want to take this opportunity to declare solemnly that the ruling party and the government will never be frightened or intimidated by the ominous world situation and will never relax in consequence of having recorded some small achievement. In other words, we shall never leave the security of our country to whims and illusions and will never base the welfare of the people on false commitments. We shall take up our national responsibility and historic task sincerely, uprightly and bravely. We shall place our feet on firm ground and move steadily and optimistically toward the goal of victory.

"Unity is strength." This is true. In history no country has ever failed provided it had one heart from top to bottom, was closely united and had moved straight and courageously toward its idealistic goal. As long as we can adhere to our objective of anti-Communism and national recovery and work hard, never relaxing and striving to the end, we are assured of success. I hope all journalists will hold high the banner of the Three Principles of the People and make more sacrifices for the country and the well-being of the people, straight-forwardly and fearlessly, so that we can hasten consummation of the great undertaking of anti-Communism and national recovery.

# Statement on U. S. Recognition of the Chinese Communist Regime

*December 16, 1978*

The decision by the United States to establish diplomatic relations with the Chinese Communist regime has not only seriously damaged the rights and interests of the Government and people of the Republic of China, but also had tremendous adverse impact upon the entire free world. For all the consequences that might arise as a result of this move, the Government of the United States alone should bear the full responsibility.

In the last few years, the United States Government has repeatedly reaffirmed its assurances to maintain diplomatic relations with the Republic of China and to honor its treaty commitments. Now that it has broken the assurances and abrogated the treaty, the United States Government cannot be expected to have the confidence of any free nations in the future.

The United States' extending diplomatic recognition to the Chinese Communist regime, which owes its very existence to terror and suppression, is not in conformity with her professed position of safeguarding human rights and strengthening the capabilities of the democratic nations so as to resist the totalitarian dictatorships. Such a move is tantamount to denying the hundreds of millions enslaved people on the Chinese mainland of their hope for an early restoration of freedom. Viewed from whatever aspects, the move by the United States constitutes a great setback to human freedom and democratic institutions. It will be condemned by all freedom-loving and peace-loving peoples over the world.

Recent international events have proven that the United States' pursuance of "normalization" process with the Chinese Communist regime did not protect the security of free Asian nations; it has further encouraged Communist subversion and aggressive activities and hastened the fall of Indochina into Communist hands. The Government and people of the Republic of China firmly believe lasting international peace and security can

置個人死生於度外

以國家興亡為己任

President Chiang repeated the counsel of President Chiang Kai-shek, his father, not to be "disquieted in time of adversity but to be firm with dignity and self-reliant with vigor" as he urged national unity following the U.S. recognition of Red China and break in formal diplomatic relations with the Republic of China.

never be established on an unstable foundation of expediency.

Regardless of how the international situation may develop, the Republic of China as a sovereign nation will, with her glorious tradition, unite all her people, civilian and military, at home and abroad, to continue her endeavors of progress in social, economic and political fields. The Chinese Government and people, faithful to the national objectives and their international responsibilities, have full confidence in the future of the Republic of China.

The late President Chiang Kai-shek had repeatedly instructed the Chinese people to be firm with dignity and to complete the task of national recovery and national reconstruction. The Government

and people of the Republic of China have the determination and faith that they will exert their utmost to work together with other free peoples in democratic countries and to counter Communist tyrannical rule and its aggressive policy. Henceforth, we shall be calm and firm, positive and hardworking. It is urged that all citizens cooperate fully with the government, with one heart and one soul, united and determined to tide over this difficult moment. Under whatever circumstances, the Republic of China will neither negotiate with the Chinese Communist regime, nor compromise with Communism, and she will never give up her sacred tasks of recovering the mainland and delivering the compatriots there. This firm position shall remain unchanged.

# Address to the Annual Constitution Day Meeting of the National Assembly

*December 25, 1978*

The 1978 Constitution Day Rally of the Republic of China, the 13th Plenary Session of the Commission for the Study of Constitutional Problems of the National Assembly and the 1978 Convention of Members of the National Assembly are holding their joint opening ceremony today. I respect you for coming here today to look into the work of the National Assembly and for the efforts of the Commission for the Study of Constitutional Problems to promote democratic and constitutional government and to plan the great undertaking of anti-Communism and national recovery.

Implementation of the Constitution has led our country into a new and constitutional era. This Constitution was brought to fruition through the struggle, sacrifice, sweat and blood of innumerable numbers of revolutionary martyrs led first by our National Founding Father, Dr. Sun Yat-sen, and then by our late President Chiang Kaishek. As we commemorate this anniversary of the Constitution by recalling the miraculous achievements of our forefathers in overcoming tens of thousands of difficulties, and as we think of the hundreds of millions of our compatriots suffering under Communist persecution on the mainland, we feel our historic sense of responsibility has become greater, especially in the face of present national difficulties. At this critical time, the inescapable need is to forge our hearts into one so that we can maintain our constitutional rule intact and ensure national security with the overwhelming power of our fortitude and the courage of our actions. I earnestly hope you will provide our people with extraordinary inspiration and our government with extraordinary support. This is required in order to rally the strength of the whole nation in overcoming the current crisis and carrying out our momentous and difficult tasks in this stage of our history.

We cannot deny that the Carter administration's betrayal in abrogating the U.S. treaty with us has dealt a heavy blow to our great undertaking of national recovery and has inflicted immeasurable damage on the free world. To safeguard our country in this developing crisis, the Executive

中華民國憲法

The Constitution of the Republic of China is one of the most modern and people-oriented in the world. Free China is pledged to return these guarantees to the mainland, where they originated in 1947.

Yuan (cabinet) decided to ask the President to adopt emergency measures by decree and take other necessary steps in accordance with the powers granted him in Article 1 of the Constitutional Temporary Provisions Effective During the Period of Communist Rebellion and thus to assure the protection of our national interests and our people's well-being. I greatly appreciate the dedicated support for this governmental action by people throughout the nation. I have been especially moved by the powerful expressions of the people's patriotism. I am further convinced that if everything is based on the Constitution and if we can advance the functions of constitutional government, we shall be able to cope with any eventuality.

In the face of the current extraordinary situation, we can expect further and even greater difficulties. We must endure humiliation, take up our heavy duties and carry out our long-term struggle with the strongest fortitude and the most enduring patience. We must undertake careful review, think things out soberly and design our counter-measures with special calm and prudence in order to advance and carry out our policy and reach our goal. We have always believed that while the objective factors of success may be decided by others, the subjective factors are always in our own hands. Looking back at the 67-year history of the Republic of China, we can see that in every struggle against foreign aggression and against domestic rebellion, we invariably have had to count on ourselves to reverse any adverse situation and to restore order through the overcoming of difficulties. In the end, we have always won out. It is a fact that since the United States declared its intention of establishing diplomatic relations with the Chinese Communists, our compatriots at home and abroad have shown their dignity and spirit of self-reliance and their devotion and solidarity with one heart and one will. This assures our success in creating a favorable objective situation through subjective struggle.

Today I must reiterate that the solemnity of the Republic of China's Constitution, which was written by representatives of the people of the whole nation, can never be diminished. As the government of the Republic of China was established in accordance with this Constitution, it follows that the government of the Republic of China is the sole legal government representing the people of the whole nation. The mainland is the territory of the Republic of China, and the government of the Republic of China will never abandon its sovereignty there. The Chinese Communist regime is a rebel entity trying to destroy the Constitution and ravage the country and people. This regime obviously cannot represent China, not to say the Chinese people. In time to come, we shall never enter into negotiations with the Chinese Communists. We shall carry out our struggle against the Communists and for national recovery to a successful conclusion.

The government of the Republic of China is determined to ensure social peace and stability, promote the people's welfare and continue the advancement of democratic government and national construction on the basis of the Constitution, and to strengthen our national authority and assure human rights. In keeping with this fundamental national policy and to maintain the security and interests of the nation and the people, we can never tolerate the existence of any statement or action that could imperil our fundamental national policy of anti-Communism and national recovery or that could undermine the foundations of our country. To augment our constitutional accomplishments, we should give priority consideration to national security and the people's interests as we adopt new measures. This is to say that we shall do all that we can in promoting anything helpful to the advancement of constitutional government and the cause of anti-Communism and national recovery, and that we shall do our utmost to eliminate anything that could hinder the advancement of constitutional government and the cause of national recovery.

Our Constitution was written on the mainland and was implemented on the mainland. As a result of the

Communist rebellion, hundreds of millions of our mainland compatriots are unable to enjoy the benefits of constitutional government. To the contrary, they are still suffering from the ravages of Communist tyranny. They have no freedom and no human rights. They have lost their human dignity. As we here in Taiwan bask in the glory of constitutionalism, we never cease to think of the mainland and our suffering compatriots there. It is our inescapable duty to destroy the Communists and recover the mainland at the earliest possible moment so as to convey the whole of the Constitution to the mainland and enable our compatriots there to join us in enjoying the fruits of constitutionalism.

You honorable members represent the people of the whole country. At this extraordinary moment for the country and at this meeting, I am sure you can set your sights even higher, think things out with care and keep the changes of the situation in mind so as to encourage the government, inspire the masses of the people, forge their hearts into one and combine all their strands of strength into one great chain. This is a requirement of attaining our constitutional goal, carrying out our anti-Communist struggle and successfully completing the unchanging historic task of national restoration and construction. Let us join in ensuring our survival with unity, construction and development.

The China Youth Corps, which President Chiang headed and helped build, has taken the lead in developing centers for youth recreation in the mountains and elsewhere. This is a ski area at Mt. Hohuan.

New Year's Day is the anniversary of the Republic of China's establishment. The nation looks forward to the President's address and student performances at the Presidential Square in Taipei.

# New Year's Day Message

*January 1, 1979*

This is New Year's Day of the 68th year of the Republic of China and also the anniversary of its founding. This is the beginning of another new year and also another milestone on our road of national construction.

Our National Founding Father, Dr. Sun Yat-sen, led the National Revolution to establish the Republic of China in order to ensure freedom and international equality for our country. Consequently, our nation goal is to build the republic of China and promote a commonwealth of great harmony through peaceful undertakings in accordance with the Three Principles of the People. Since the founding of our country, we have always embraced this spirit and adhered to the lofty characteristics of the Chinese people as we have concentrated and advanced benevolence and safeguarded justice to fulfill our responsibility for maintaining national independence and promoting world peace. In the last 68 years, we have suffered from domestic adversity and external aggression. Yet without exception, we have defeated all of our enemies. Under the brilliant and selfless Three Principles of the People, our national flag of Blue Sky and White Sun continues to fly high across the world.

### History

Although the history of the Republic of China is fraught with distress and hardship, history shows that our country has never bowed to either distress or hardship, nor have we ever surrendered to the enemy. Since the establishment of our country, enemies have included countless warlords, imperialists of various countries and now the most vicious and also the last of all, the Chinese Communist regime. The decisive weapon in countering and defeating the enemy is adherence to the 5,000-year-old dauntless spirit of the Chinese people and the perfect excellence of Chinese culture. We have always stood on the side of truth and justice, and so we have always been victorious. In the past, we wiped out the warlords and defeated the imperialists in order to win national independence and safeguard our 5,000-year-old history and culture. In the last half century, our determined anti-Communism has safeguarded our nation's independence, freedom and time-honored history and culture. We have fought against the ravaging and extinction of our great traditions by the non-Chinese of Communism. We may say that our war against Communism is basically for the protection of our people and our culture.

## Usurpation

What have the Chinese Communists been doing in the 30 years since their usurpation of the mainland? Their immorality and iniquity are beyond description. To epitomize, the people have struggled ceaselessly and faced endless bloodletting only to be rewarded with lives of deprivation and terror filled with misery and despair. Their properties have been confiscated, their families have been destroyed, their relatives have been separated from them and they have lost human dignity, freedom and their rights. The whole of the mainland has been plunged into a dark era unparalleled in history. Having succeeded in ravaging the mainland people, the Chinese Communists are now engaged in international united front activities in an attempt to establish links with the free world. They have blatantly clamored for so-called "modernization." This ploy either testifies to the bankruptcy of Communism or is a lie to cheat the people of the world and deceive the international politicians in the hope of consolidating Communism's tyrannical rule. The victims continue to be the Chinese people. The only hope for our despairing compatriots is the recovery of the mainland by the government of the Republic of China and the glorious restoration of the Three Principles of the People to our once hallowed land. The responsibility of carrying out the historic task of recovering the mainland and delivering from Communist slavery and tyranny compatriots whose blood is the same as ours rests squarely on the shoulders of each of the 17 million people who live in this free bastion of national revival — Taiwan, Penghu, Kinmen and Matsu — under the democratic and constitutional government of the Three Principles of the People, and also on the shoulders of each of the 20 million anti-Communist overseas Chinese. Our success will enable our compatriots to share our life of stability, peace, happiness and well-being.

Consequently, our anti-Communist struggle will never cease until Communism is eliminated from Chinese territory and until the Chinese Communist regime has been destroyed. We are sure that any insurgent organization which runs contrary to the wishes and the will of the Chinese people and any evil force inconsistent with Chinese

On New Year's Day of 1979, President Chiang reminded the people that although the Republic was beset by adversity, Chinese sages had long ago pointed out that a country can thrive on distress. The Chinese have shown their unity and patriotism with one will and one heart, he told compatriots, and are prepared to surmount all barriers.

tradition will never be accepted or tolerated by the Chinese people and are bound to fail. Although the objective situation may sometimes follow a course unfavorable to us, we must carry on our struggle to final victory.

### Strength

We do not deny that our country is again distressed and assaulted by adversity. But our ancient sages have told us that a country thrives on distress. We can see today that all of our compatriots at home and abroad have demonstrated with one will and one heart their absolute unity and patriotism. They have manifested our intrepid national founding spirit to the full. This attests that we can truly be firm with dignity and persevere with fortitude. This also attests that we can grow despite distress. So long as we maintain our confidence and the revolutionary vigor and fortitude that obtained at the time of our national founding, we can cope with any challenge, stand up under any test, overcome any difficulty and surmount any barrier on the way to success.

Our President Chiang Kai-shek told us: "No one can make light of us if we can hold our heads high. No one can bully us if we can make ourselves strong. No one can cheat us if we can have confidence in ourselves. No one can overcome us if we can stand on our own feet." Beginning today, we must use our own heads and our own strength, and redouble our efforts

to hold our heads high and further our own confidence. We must stand on our own feet and rely on ourselves as we face the new struggle and write a new page in our history.

As to the ways of self-support and self-reliance, I think it is fundamental that we strengthen our psychological preparedness in addition to improving our national defenses, developing our economic projects and augmenting our tangible national development projects. Psychological preparedness equates to spiritual development. We must arouse the conscience of all and work hard to "revolutionize" our minds. This will establish our people's independent mental foundation and strengthen the resiliency of their staying power in time of hardship.

All of us love our country, all of us will sacrifice for our country and all of us will come forward to save our country. We shall encourage this total patriotism of our people and forge them into a massive force of national salvation. This is the first step in development of our movement to enhance the national spirit.

We shall rid ourselves of the psychology of dependence, discard the mentality of chance, discredit illusions and be determined to shape our own course and encourage our zeal to sacrifice for the nation by arousing our awareness of the dictates of conscience.

### Will

Whether we come from the north, the south, the east or the west, and whether we are men or women, old or young, we have a common will and must be honest with each other. We must unite and share in our joys and sorrows, even as passengers aboard a boat sailing through stormy seas. We must agree on our concepts and take concerted steps to overcome the crisis. This is the only way to succeed in the struggle against Communism and for national salvation.

On this day, our country and people have reached the critical moment of life or death. The government is determined to do its utmost to provide for the security of our country and our society, and to promote the well-being of our people on the basis of constitutional rule. The government is wholly determined to remove all factors and phenomena obstructing the fulfillment of this goal. We have the sincerity and confidence to carry out our duty and to safeguard our country and our people. No obstacle can obstruct our march. We shall never allow any pressure to alter our unchangeable course.

At this beginning of the new year and of nature's seasonal renewal, we are optimistic and courageous, enthusiastic and adventurous. We are determined to make our greatest contributions to the cause of national recovery and against Communism and so to grasp new opportunities to assure our victory.

Let us pray for the prosperity of the Republic of China!

I wish you good health and happiness. You must take care of yourselves for the benefit of the country.

# Dialogue with René Viénet, Special Envoy, L'Express

*January 2, 1979*

I. On U.S. "normalization of relations" with the Chinese Communist regime

*Q1. Were you surprised at U.S. announcement of "normalization of relations" with the Chinese Communist regime?*

A. The "Shanghai Communique" of 1972 signed by Richard Nixon and Chou En-lai said the United States intended to seek "normalization" of relations between the two parties. But afterward the United States sent an envoy to the Repub-

lic of China to explain that "normalization" did not mean the establishment of diplomatic relations. The United States repeatedly pledged, both publicly and privately, to continue the diplomatic relations and honor the mutual defense treaty with the Republic of China.

During the period between Nixon's 1972 visit to the mainland and U.S. announcement of intention to establish diplomatic relations with the Chinese Communist regime, the United States declared, at least 20 times, that it would maintain friendship and diplomatic relations with the Republic of China and honor the mutual defense treaty. The United States also said it would not discuss another country's destiny behind its back.

I must point out that the Republic of China and the United States have had a long-standing diplomatic and cooperative relationship. During the Second World War, the two countries fought shoulder to shoulder. We signed a mutual defense treaty in 1954. This further strengthened our alliance and made tremendous contributions to the peace and security of the Asian-Pacific region. Although there have been new developments in the region since the treaty was signed, the Chinese Communist threat to Asian peace is more serious than any time before. To ensure peace and security in the Asian-Pacific region and to contain Chinese Communist expansion, the ROC-U.S. mutual defense treaty not only has benefited the Republic of China but is also essential to the permanent interest of the United States and the free world. So the United

110

States had no reason to abrogate this treaty unilaterally.

The United States is known for its tradition of safeguarding freedom and human rights. I want to ask why the United States chose to establish diplomatic relations with Red China just as people the world over were accusing the Chinese Communists of killing many innocent people, ravaging human rights and depriving people of their freedom? I also want to ask why the United States should have decided to "normalize relations" with the Chinese Communists at a time when the people on the mainland are putting up posters to demand the restoration of their freedom? The United States claims to practice democracy and promote the rule of law. Why should President Carter betray us so soon after Congress had passed a resolution expressing the attachment of great importance to the ROC-U.S. defense treaty. The United States always hopes its allies will implement democracy. Then, why did the United States announce its decision on recognizing the Chinese Communist regime as we were preoccupied with elections for additional members of our central parliamentary organizations?

In its 202-year history, the United States has never failed to keep its treaty obligations. The Republic of China also has always kept its treaty commitments. At this critical moment of our country, we never thought that one of our sworn allies could forsake its treaty of alliance overnight. Frankly, we were much surprised at the sudden announcement of the abrogation of the treaty.

*Q2. According to President Carter's announcement, the Sino-American mutual defense treaty is still valid for another year, and in the past your country has always tried to strengthen your defense system. If the treaty expires, is there any possibility for you to obtain from the United States the latest defensive weapons?*

A. In the face of the Chinese Communist threat, we have always given first priority to the strengthening of our national defenses. We have continued to modernize our weapons and other defense equipment. Under these new circumstances, we certainly shall continue to modernize our weapons. We need better and faster planes and vessels to strengthen our sea and air defenses. In the past, we have ceaselessly tried to procure the most modern weapons from the United States, but failed to get all that we wanted. To ensure Taiwan's security, it is the future responsibility of the United States to sell us the latest and most sophisticated weapons.

*Q3. Besides the United States, do you obtain weapons from any other countries? Does your country plan to diversify the sources of conventional weapons?*

A. Because of the mutual defense treaty and our military alliance with the United States, we have in the past obtained most of our weapons from the United States. From now on, we shall continue to try to buy American weapons.

*Q4. The United States has pledged to maintain other treaties than the mutual defense treaty.*

*For a country that unilaterally severs diplomatic ties and still pledges to maintain technical, cultural, economic, scientific, commercial & other relations, do you think such pledges are credible? When the U.S. guarantees that the Chinese Communists will not come out to make harassment, do you think it has made secret arrangements with the Chinese Communist regime?*

A. Because of many years of friendship and alliance, the United States and the Republic of China have developed close relations in many fields. The maintenance of cultural, technical, economic and trade relations are in the interest of both countries. However, we are not content with this. It is our position that the two countries should continue to maintain full relations. We think this view is consistent with the interests of the U.S. Congress, mass communication media and broad masses of the people.

President Carter's announcement of intention to sever diplomatic relations with the Republic of China elicited strong reactions from Congress, the press and the people. The White House announced that sentiment expressed after the announcement was 4 to 1 in our favor, indicating the deep friendship for the Republic of China. In keeping with our traditional friendship, I hope members of Congress and the American people will urge the U.S. Government to continue to strengthen its cultural, technical, scientific and trade relations with us, sell us more sophisticated weapons and further political relations in order to enhance our security.

*Q5. Do you think the U.S. embassy in Taipei would be replaced by a liaison office or a more informal organization?*

A. To maintain Sino-American friendship and security, cultural, economic and other close relations, we believe appropriate arrangements should be made.

*Q6. Do you think the Chinese Communists are able to invade Taiwan?*

A. To invade Taiwan militarily is the unchanging policy of the Chinese Communist regime and has been written into its constitution. Nevertheless, because of our strong military defenses, the Chinese Communists have never dared to make such an attempt. Now they are increasing their military striking power. To prepare for any eventuality, we hope to continue obtaining the latest-model weapons from the United States so as to increase our defense capability.

II. On the situation of the Chinese Communist regime

*Q1. You have said that when the Chinese Communists seek for negotiations, we should not believe them because negotiation to them is just the first step of war. But what do you think of a Chinese Communist overture to make economic exchange through Hongkong?*

A. Our position is that regardless of the circumstances, we shall not negotiate with the Chinese Communists. Nor shall we enter into any other forms of contact with them.

*Q2. Admitting that you have negated the sincerity of the Chinese Communists in seeking Chinese reunification by peaceful means, what is your assessment of Teng Hsiao-ping in comparison with the "Gang of Four"?*

A. Some foreigners like to use such terms as "radicals," "moderates" and "pragmatists" to distinguish among Chinese Communist leaders. These distinctions are superficial. Mao Tse-tung and Chou En-lai, Hua Kuo-feng and Teng Hsiao-ping are all jackals from the same lair. In substance, they are all Communists without material differences.

*Q3. Do you think there will be changes in the Chinese Communist regime as in Yugoslavia?*

A. Soviet Russia and the Chinese Communist regime have been pursuing their conspiracy of conquering the world through "proletarian revolution." This has never changed. As the Chinese Communists are in an inferior position, they have resorted to dialectical Machiavelianism in an attempt to pit their secondary enemy against their archenemy by pretending to be nationalists and wooing the United States. As soon as they have attained their goal, the friends today will become the enemies tomorrow. Although the Chinese Communists have sought to give the impression that they are changing after the pattern of Yugoslavia, theirs continues to be a regime of class struggle and oppression of the people.

III. On social and political activities in Taiwan

*Q1. Taiwan has taken a group of Vietnamese refugees. Is it prepared to take more? It has become clearer and clearer that most of the refugees who have fled Vietnam by ships are ethnic Chinese.*

A. On the basis of humanity, our government is deeply concerned about the people suffering under Communist rule in Vietnam. We have brought some refugees to Taiwan through the International Red Cross. The government has cared for these people and helped them return to a normal life of study and employment. This help is continuing. With regard to the Vietnamese refugees, we know that the French have extended a helping hand. We hope this humanitarian gesture will be continued. At the same time, France should condemn the Vietnamese Communists for violating human rights.

René Viénet from L'Express of Paris was told by President Chiang that the people of France should carry on their great tradition of liberty, equality and human rights so as to help others gain freedom.

Housing for the people is a major goal of the government. With land and construction costs rising, President Chiang has urged the allocation of more funds for public housing. Some of the units are rented and the rest are sold on easy terms.

*Q2. Your Constitution provides for two representative systems. Local representatives are elected regularly and many Kuomintang and independent candidates have participated in the elections. In the National Assembly and the Legislative Yuan, however, most of the members were elected before 1949 except for a few from Taiwan. Why do you maintain two systems of representation? Or do you still believe in the possibility of recovering the mainland?*

A. The Republic of China is a democratic and constitutional country in which all elections are held in accordance with the Constitution. In addition to local elections at all levels, we hold elections for additional members to central level parliamentary organizations and to fill vacancies at the national level.

IV. On relations with France

*Q1. There is not any organization, even an informal and cultural one, that represents France in Taiwan. Do you encourage the establishment of a French cultural organization in Taiwan, like the Germany Cultural Center or the Interchange Association of Japan to engage in such activities as religion, exhibition and screening motion pictures?*

A. France has a long cultural history and French culture has always been highly regarded in the world, including the Republic of China. To strengthen relations between our two countries, the people of the Republic of China would be glad to see France establish in our country an organization to engage in cultural, trade and tourism activities. This would be very helpful in promoting contacts and understanding between the two peoples. Some of our colleges and universities have French language and literature departments and many graduates pursue advanced studies in France. Some French students are studying in Taiwan. These gratifying developments have contributed greatly to friendship between our countries.

*Q2. Do you have any message for the French people?*

A. France is a freedom-loving country with long and glorious traditions. The French people are one of the most civilized peoples of the world. When we read Western history, we are inspired by the spirit shown by the French people in their struggle for liberty, equality and human rights. I strongly hope that the French people will carry on and further glorify this great tradition so as to inspire others who are struggling for survival and freedom and against totalitarianism and slavery. I hope the French people will unite with the truly peace-loving democratic countries and peoples.

It is regrettable that there is no official relationship between France and the Republic of China. But this does not mean there is no contact between our two peoples. The French people have shown great interest in and concern about Oriental and traditional Chinese culture. I hope they will increase their understanding of Oriental culture as represented by the Republic of China and promote friendship between our two peoples.

# Statement after Establishment of the Coordination Council for North American Affairs

*February 15, 1979*

After the government of the Republic of China announced establishment of an organization to administer new relations with the United States, President Chiang Ching-kuo addressed the following statement to the people of the nation:

The unilateral announcement of the U.S. government last December 15 terminating diplomatic relations with us and recognizing the tyrannical Chinese Communists was a historic tragedy affecting the whole world. In the last two months, we have endured the heavy pain in our hearts in order to negotiate and talk with the United States amidst danger and concern. We wanted to do all we could to mitigate damage from the tragedy and protect the interest of the country and people. In this period, we have done everything we could to carry out our country's fundamental policy. We especially appreciate the support of our compatriots at home and abroad. From beginning to end, they have trusted and encouraged the government and have contributed their wisdom and assistance to the country. We also have been deeply moved by the voice of justice persistently heard in the U.S. Congress and among the multitudes of the American people. This voice has given us warm sympathy and support. It has expressed the profound friendship between the peoples of the Republic of China and the United States and at the same time has indicated that justice still prevails.

In order to restructure and seek the continued development of relations between our two countries, we have decided to set up a new organization. Reality requires that this time-honored and extremely close relationship be perpetuated, so we must swallow the bitter and handle the situation with all the fortitude at our command. We are also show-

ing the Chinese people's ability to overcome extreme hardship with maximum courage and perseverance. As the negotiations between the two countries proceed, I must emphasize to all the people of the nation that the Republic of China's fundamental policy of anti-Communism and national recovery will never be changed. Current difficulties can in no way shake our confidence and determination. To the contrary, we shall execute our national policy more vigorously, courageously and determinedly. Politically, we shall remain in the democratic camp and safeguard human rights. Economically, we shall strengthen our construction program to sustain steady growth. Militarily, we shall fortify national defense to ensure national security. As long as we remain unafraid, do what we should, maintain our optimism and self-

confidence and uphold our position with self-reliance, we can turn adversity to our advantage, open up a fresh vista and create a new horizon.

With the weighty mandate of the people and in the face of national danger and difficulty, I have steadfastly urged myself to proceed with caution and courage and have never allowed myself the illusion that I can afford a single moment of negligence or laxity. I appreciate wholeheartedly the people's total and unreserved support of the government. I want to pledge anew that I shall contribute all that I have and join with my compatriots in partaking of both joy and sorrow. I shall unite with them indestructibly to carry out our common ideal and reach our common goal. We must march forward together courageously until we have won the final victory.

Yehliu on the northern coast is a scenic spot of rugged grandeur symbolizing the indomitable spirit of the free Chinese people. President Chiang has called upon these people to "create a new horizon."

# Address at the United Overseas Chinese Anti-Communist Convention

*February 27, 1979*

Overseas Chinese have suffered heavily at the hands of the Communists and have joined forces in giving strong support to the anti-Communist movement the world over. President Chiang has taken a deep interest in these activities.

Ladies and Gentlemen:

As representatives of the overseas Chinese people throughout the world, you have returned to the free motherland from various places to attend this anti-Communist convention and jointly formulate a policy for national salvation. This fact alone gives evidence that the children of China are united as one flesh and blood and share common interests. This meeting is an expression of our lasting solidarity and a means of further honoring your enduring patriotism.

The overseas Chinese are the mother of revolution. Since the Republic of China's establishment, our history has attested to the identity of the "overseas Chinese" with Chinese "patriotism." When we mention the "overseas Chinese," we naturally think of their patriotic conduct; when we consider their patriotic conduct, we naturally think of their participation. This traditional link between the overseas Chinese and patriotism assumes especially deep meaning today at a time when our country needs the cooperative endeavors of people at home and abroad in order to survive.

### Courage and wisdom

All of us are clearly aware that the U.S. decision to establish diplomatic relations with the Chinese Communists is a major reverse in mankind's quest for freedom and democracy. This has made our great undertaking of national recovery and reconstruction more difficult. At the same time, this gives us the opportunity to demonstrate our courage and wisdom and to test our resolve and confidence. So long as we can stand up under this grinding trial, harden our fortitude and augment our strength through self-reliance, we shall be able to overcome any difficulty and reach any goal.

We are absolutely determined to break through all obstacles, overcome all difficulties, smash all Chinese Communist infiltrations and attempts to divide us, and fortify our anti-Communist camp for national recovery. We shall at the same time confirm the goals of our endeavors, vigorously implement the Three Principles of

the People, accelerate national construction and finally apply the framework and the fruit of our benevolent rule and construction in this bastion of national recovery to every part of our lost territory. When this is accomplished, all of our compatriots will be able to join with us in enjoying a free, democratic, peaceful and equalitarian way of life.

**Contributions to nation**

Overseas Chinese all over the

The President told overseas Chinese visiting the Republic of China that the increase in visits from those living abroad has greatly encouraged the nation and people. "We all share the same joys, sorrows, honor and humiliation," he said.

world have made unceasing spiritual and physical contributions in carrying out this historic task. Their enthusiasm in making contributions has grown steadily. This great tradition is to be seen in the annual increase in the number of overseas Chinese visitors, their augmented investment in productive enterprises here at home, their insistent and courageous resistance to Chinese Communist united front temptations, and especially in their active moral and physical support of the government in their motherland during the last two months. This stand has touched the chords of each motherland heart and raised the confidence of all.

The Ten Major Construction Projects have been completed one after another in this bastion of freedom. Now the Twelve New Projects are being successively undertaken. Political renovation and social construction are vigorously promoted. All of this requires the full support of our compatriots abroad. We know that the overseas Chinese and the motherland share the same joys and sorrows, the same honor and humility. A prosperous and powerful motherland is the cherished wish of all the overseas Chinese of the earth. We must treasure and sustain their patriotism and reinforce our efforts for national recovery in the struggle against Communism. We must unite the children of China under the Flag of Blue Sky and White Sun and move forward together in the march to eradicate Communist tyranny, implement freedom and democracy and reconstruct a united and powerful new China.

### Evil Communists

At this moment, however, we must give particular attention to the fact that the Chinese Communists are deceiving the world with their clamor for peaceful unification. Actually, they are tightening the screws on our mainland compatriots' hope of freedom. At the same time, they are going to any lengths to step up sabotage and subversion against the free motherland and subjecting the overseas Chinese to coercion and trickery in their effort to split and weaken us. We must heighten our vigilance and fortify our psychological defenses. All of us know that every Chinese wants the lasting solidarity of the people and peace for the country, true political freedom and democracy, and a stable and affluent life. We must therefore attract the attention of the people of the world and expose the intrigues and hypocrisy of the Communists. When this is accomplished, the Chinese Communists will no longer be able to conceal their evil nature and will be ostracized by the people of the world.

### Admiration

I should like to take this opportunity to express my admiration for the contributions of the overseas Chinese, to identify our common goals and to explain our faith and determination to all the overseas Chinese of the world. I have confidence that your meeting here will intensify our faith and determination and cement our solidarity in the struggle against Communism and in our efforts to strengthen ourselves through self-reliance. This will elevate the patriotic tradition and glorious accomplishments of the overseas Chinese to a new and brilliant level. Finally, I want to wish all of you happiness and great success for this meeting.

# Dialogue with Benno Kroll, Reporter, GEO Magazine, West Germany

*March 28, 1979*

*Q1. Mr. President, the Chinese in the Republic of China on Taiwan have more freedom, more affluence and more social equality than during any other period and under any other Chinese government. Regretfully, only a minority of your people have the privilege to enjoy these circumstances. Which are the political prerequisites so that one day all Chinese can live like those on Taiwan? Which domestic policies on the mainland? Which foreign policies in the world?*

A. I appreciate your question. I can see you have a deep under-

standing of the situation of the Republic of China in Taiwan and that you are concerned with the future of the Chinese people. We are deeply convinced that before all Chinese can enjoy the freedom, prosperity and social equality evident in Taiwan, we first must root out Communism from the Chinese mainland. We firmly believe this is the common aspiration of the Chinese people in Taiwan, overseas and on the mainland. Under Chinese Communist tyranny, the people on the mainland have been deprived of all freedoms and human rights and are leading inhuman lives. We are striving to carry out policies based on the Three Principles of the People and reconstruct Taiwan as a model province of the Republic of China. When the mainland people come to understand these policies, they will rise up, topple the Chinese Communist regime and attain freedom and democracy.

*Q2. Do you believe, just as your honorable father, President Chiang Kai-shek, that the Chinese mainland can be militarily recovered? Do you believe that such a military conflict can be localized in China or do you see the danger, that this conflict could spark a new world war?*

A. The late President Chiang pointed out that the mainland could be recovered through efforts that were "70 per cent political and 30 per cent military." We do not rely completely on military strength to recover the mainland. As I have already said, we are building in Taiwan a democratic and free society based on the Three Principles of the People, and our accomplishments will have a significant political impact on the people of the mainland. The Chinese Communists seek to perpetuate their rule through totalitarian persecution and this has earned them the bitter hatred of all the people. Therefore, our effort to recover the mainland is in fulfillment of the people's wish. Any action that helps the mainland people eliminate tyrannical Chinese Communist control and the few Chinese Communist leaders will receive enthusiastic support from the mainland people and will not lead to world war.

*Q3. If you intend to re-establish the Three Principles of Dr. Sun Yat-sen and of the Kuomintang on the Chinese mainland, which nations, in your opinion, would be your allies?*

A. To reconstruct a unified, free and democratic China on the mainland based on the Three Principles of the People will not only contribute to Asian stability but also safeguard world peace. Our efforts therefore should be supported by all freedom-loving countries of the world. I believe no country will interfere with these efforts.

*Q4. It is my personal conviction that the Chinese people on Taiwan are not wholly responsible for their political situation, but rather, that the responsibility must be shared by the Western nations. I will make this conviction very clear in my article. In this context, I am interested in your opinion about the foreign affairs of the Republic of China. Can the Republic of China be politically effective without diplomatic relations with the nations of Western Europe? Or is it sufficient that these relations are reduced primarily to economical and cultural ones?*

A. It is regrettable that the Republic of China has no diplomatic relations with many Western European countries. This is not only a loss to our country but also to the free nations of Europe. The continuous existence of the Republic of China, its steady increase in strength and especially rapid economic growth and the raising of the people's standard of living, should have led the Western European countries to understand that the ROC's political, economic and social systems based on freedom and democracy are totally different from those of Chinese Communist totalitarianism and slavery. I am glad to note that the Western European countries have gradually increased their substantive relations with us. I hope they will come to understand further the aspiration of all the Chinese for freedom and democracy and their efforts to attain these goals.

*Q5. Which domestic reforms are to be expected for the Republic of China in the near future?*

A. The government of the Republic of China will continue to implement democratic constitutional rule, strengthen economic construction, raise the people's standard of living and narrow the gap between rich and poor in accordance with established national policy. The purpose is to seek a better life for the Chinese people — not only in Taiwan, Penghu, Kinmen and Matsu but also on the mainland.

Benno Kroll came from GEO Magazine of West Germany. President Chiang told him that Western European countries were gradually increasing "substantial relations" with the Republic of China.

# Dialogue with James D. Cary, Correspondent, the Copley News Service

*April 15, 1979*

*Q1. U.S. recognition of the People's Republic of China has raised a number of questions about the future welfare and security of the Republic of China.*

*Do you anticipate that you will have to defend your nation against a Communist Chinese military attack at some time in the future? If so, how soon?*

A. The Chinese Communists have written the goal of invading Taiwan into their constitution. The timing of their invasion depends on the defensive capability of the Republic of China. They may advance the timetable to externalize their internal turmoil. The Republic of China must therefore develop national defense science, modernize its weapons and equipment and maintain a high level of vigilance so as to safeguard our own security and deal heavy blows to the Chinese Communists in the event of attack.

*Q2. Can the Republic of China win such a battle?*

A. The Republic of China has continuously stressed national defense in past years. Our armed forces have excellent morale and have been strictly trained and reorganized. The government and people are confident of successfully defending Taiwan, Penghu, Kinmen and Matsu. However, we know the free countries must cooperate and help one another in order to cope with the aggressive expansion of international Communism. We hope the United States will provide us with sufficient defensive weapons to strengthen our military position.

*Q3. Do you see any prospect of negotiations with the People's Republic to settle the differences between your two governments?*

A. Our position is firmly

opposed to talks or contacts with the Chinese Communists. Since U.S. establishment of diplomatic relations with Peiping, the Chinese Communists have stepped up their "peaceful unification" propaganda to attain a goal that cannot be attained by force. We shall not fall into the Chinese Communist trap. Negotiations also are proscribed by the necessity of providing democracy-loving Chinese at home and abroad and freedom-seeking compatriots on the mainland with a model for the reconstruction of China and to make sure no one concludes we have given up our struggle for freedom and democracy.

*Q4. Even if negotiations aimed at an overall settlement are not possible, is there a possibility that you might engage in talks on restoring certain mutually beneficial services such as mail, cultural and economic exchanges, reuniting families or even having your athletes participate jointly with Communist Chinese athletes in international competitions?*

A. Considering that the Chinese Communists have denied the people all the basic freedoms, any assertion that mainland people can now communicate with the outside world is a lie. Communication between the peoples on the two sides of the Taiwan Straits via mail and cultural and commercial exchanges is possible only if the

One of the Ten Major Construction Projects originated and backed by President Chiang is the China Shipbuilding Corporation yard at Kaohsiung. The drydock of 1 million tons capacity is the world's second biggest.

Chinese Communists get rid of Communism, establish a free economy and restore democracy based on the Three Principles of the People.

The Chinese mainland is a closed society while the Republic of China is an open one. Exchanges would only provide the Chinese Communists with opportunities for infiltration and subversion.

The people on the mainland are compatriots and blood relatives. Although we will have no contacts or talks with the Peiping regime, we have never failed to support the people's anti-Communist activities on the mainland and the common struggle to overthrow the tyrannical regime and restore freedom.

**Q5. If a negotiated settlement is not possible, and you are faced with a long period of no-war, no-peace with the Mainland, what will be the main thrust of your foreign policy in seeking national security?**

A. The foreign policy of the Republic of China provides for "remaining in the democratic camp." We believe freedom and democracy constitute the mainstream of human progress while Communism and totalitarianism are passing phenomena. We believe the goal of restoring freedom to our mainland compatriots will sooner or later be attained. In foreign policy and other aspects of national life, we shall try to open up a new horizon in relations with friendly countries and all freedom-loving, democracy-loving and peace-loving peoples of the world, and also add to our political and economic achievements and develop our way of life. Based on these accomplishments, we shall strengthen our vigorous political call to the mainland people, join ranks with them in the anti-Communist struggle so as to overthrow Chinese Communist tyranny and help them regain freedom, and construct a new China based on the Three Principles of the People. We shall also pool our efforts to assure peace, security and prosperity in the Asian and Pacific region and the whole world.

**Q6. Do you anticipate your nation will have a difficult time obtaining the arms it will need to adequately defend itself?**

A. We will try our best to overcome any difficulties. I want to point out that the Republic of China in Taiwan has been the main stabilizing force for sea and air navigational safety between Northeast Asia and Southeast Asia. With U.S. unilateral abrogation of the ROC-U.S. Mutual Defense Treaty, Red China and the Soviet Union can be expected to take advantage of the situation created by the United States to seize control of a passage which is vital to the prosperity and stability of the Asian and Pacific region, and also try to expand their spheres of influence. The consequence will upset the strategic balance in the region and injure the non-Communist countries of Asia and the Pacific as well as the United States. We hope the countries concerned will add up the merits and demerits of the situation and promptly provide us with the necessary defensive weapons to ensure the peace and security of the region.

*Q7. Will the defensive arms the United States has promised to sell you be sufficient for your needs? If not, where will you be able to obtain the weapons you require? What are the weapons you need most?*

A. In the past the United States concentrated on supplying weapons for land operations. The Republic of China now urgently requires weapons to ensure our naval supremacy and air superiority. We need modern anti-submarine equipment and high performance aircraft. The types and numbers of weapons should be sufficient to defend Taiwan, Penghu, Kinmen and Matsu and should be provided on the basis of respect for our position. We hope the United States will continue to sell us weapons to satisfy our needs. At the same time, we are continuously seeking to produce more defensive weapons for ourselves.

*Q8. Mr. President, one of the crucial issues imbedded in all this is whether your nation may turn toward the Soviet Union as a future source of military equipment, particularly the key items you may require, and whether a new relationship between the Republic of China and the Soviet Union might evolve from the present situation. Could you address this issue? The Republic of China has obviously been placed in a very difficult situation and I assume is under heavy pressures and requirements for its future security that are difficult for Americans to understand and fully grasp. Your view of how you secure your future in a hostile environment would be a major contribution to your projection of foreign policy and to our understanding the future prospects for peace in the Pacific region.*

A. The Soviet Union abetted and assisted the Chinese Communist rebellion in China. The Republic of China, which has been victimized by the Communists for 50 years, will not accept the idea that "the enemies of enemies are friends."

In foreign affairs, the Republic of China will adhere to its anti-Communist national policy, remain in the democratic camp and continue to make positive contributions to world peace and security based on moral courage and the spirit of justice. We shall strengthen total diplomacy, expand economic and technological cooperation with countries having diplomatic relations with us to further consolidate bilateral relations, and further develop economic, trade, cultural and other substantial relations through various channels with non-Communist countries having no diplomatic relations with us.

*Q9. Would you accept military and economic aid from the Soviet Union if it should be offered?*

A. As I have said before, the Republic of China has always adhered to its anti-Communist position and will not enter into any relationships with the Soviet Union. We shall remain in the democratic camp and go on fighting to safeguard the democratic and free way of life. Recent expressions of sympathy and support from the broad masses of the American people and the U.S. Congress have been very encouraging to us.

*Q10. The People's Republic of China has been outlining a major economic expansion for the past several months. It has the goal of making Mainland China into a modern industrial nation by the turn of the century. There have been some estimates it will invest 600-billion by 1985 to accomplish this. You have an intimate knowledge of the economic situation on the mainland. Do you believe the Peking regime can (1) obtain that amount of investment capital to finance such an expansion? (2) pay for a major expansion when it has so few goods to sell to the rest of the world? (3) develop the technicians, scientists and educated population needed to handle such an expansion? (4) remain stable enough politically to follow through on such an ambitious expansion program?*

A. Regarding the first question, the Chinese Communists cannot even satisfy the basic material needs of the 900 million mainland Chinese. Obviously, they cannot raise this fund by themselves; they have to rely on foreign loans. But I think that when foreign financial institutions gain a better understanding of their insolvency and the unstable regime, they will be more cautious. It will be difficult for the Chinese Communists to get massive credit.

Regarding the second question, Communist China's exports are confined to agricultural, mineral and some low-value industrial products. Last year, their exports totaled only US$12 billion. This amount will buy some foodstuffs and consumer goods, but not nearly enough for large imports of machinery and equipment. The Chinese Communists' so-called "Economic Construction Plan" requires investment of US$85 billion annually through 1985. Judging by the gap between foreign exchange and required investment, the Communists will not be able to pay for what they buy. Communist China says it is prepared to provide oil to repay loans. But how large are the oil reserves on the Chinese mainland? How much oil is available for drilling? When will there be a massive supply of oil for export? The answers to these questions are not known.

As for the third question, by Communist China's estimate, as of 1985, 800,000 scientists and technicians will be needed. The total is now only half of that. The "cultural revolution" undermined the whole educational system: schools were forced to close down; intellectuals were persecuted; the quality of education slumped. At present the equipment in schools is outdated and good teachers are few and far between. Though the Chinese Communists will send students abroad, this cannot alleviate the present urgent need. One of the thorniest problems facing the Chinese Communists is the lack of scientists and technicians so indispensable to economic construction. This shortage cannot be solved in the short run.

Regarding the fourth question, everyone knows the Peiping regime espouses the philosophy of class struggle; perpetual struggle is a means of sustaining the regime. In the two years since the death of Mao, power struggle has occurred at the higher levels on several occasions. The Chinese Communists cannot maintain political stability for long. This will make it impossible to carry out the "Economic Construction Plan" on an all-out basis.

I believe the so-called "Economic Construction Plan" of the Chinese Communists is another propaganda ploy of the Communist ruling elite to consolidate its leadership, grind down the faces of the people and bamboozle the outside world.

*Q11. Your nation has made excellent economic progress in the last 20 years. Is your boom over? What further expansion do you see? Can the Republic of China remain independent, prosperous and secure given the situation that now exists with the People's Republic of China?*

A. In the last 20 years and more, the Republic of China has been promoting a series of economic construction plans. At present, we are in the fourth year of our first Six-Year Plan. In the last few years, we have completed most of the Ten Major Construction Projects, including the North-South Freeway. Such projects as railway electrification and nuclear power plants are near completion. Now 12 more projects are under way to raise industry to a higher level, modernize agriculture and further improve communications and transportation.

Our efforts in 1978 resulted in record growth of 12.8 per cent. Per capita income topped US$-1,400. Exports, imports and industrial production hit all-time highs. Price stability was maintained. It is safe to say that our economy is booming without loss of stability.

Despite their four modernizations and efforts to isolate us diplomatically and economically, the Chinese Communists will be balked in the conspiracy. We have trade relations with more than 140 countries and areas. Our foreign trade was US$23.7 billion in 1978. The Republic of China is the eighth ranking trade partner of the United States, the fourth largest market for Japanese exports and the 19th country in world trade, excluding the OPEC nations. With this foundation, I am confident the Republic of China will maintain its security and prosperity.

*Q12. A final question, Mr. President: The People's Republic has been swept by periodic political upheavals. Mr. Teng, the present strongman, is 74 and will not live forever. Do you anticipate more political turmoil on the mainland? What will happen after Teng is gone?*

A. More political turmoil is in prospect on the Chinese mainland whether Teng lives or dies. The power struggle among the higher-ups in Communist China, the conflicts and crises involved in implementing the four modernizations and the discontent of tens of millions of rusticated youths, coupled with demands for a higher standard of living from the broad masses of workers and farmers, will give rise to an anti-Communist tide on the mainland and fuel hopes for freedom, democracy and a better life. All this must lead to political turmoil.

# Address at Monthly Sun Yat-sen Memorial Service

*April 20, 1979*

For all Chinese, December 16, 1978, is an unforgettable date. This was a day that brought trauma to our hearts and made us realize the necessity of striving to the utmost for self-reliance. The shock to our hearts resulted from the actions of the government of the United States, leader of the free world, in mistaking an enemy for a friend and establishing diplomatic relations with the Chinese Communists, who have illegally occupied the Chinese mainland for 30 years, massacred a countless number of people and posed a continuous threat to world peace. At the same time, the United States severed diplomatic relations with the Republic of China, a cooperative friend of long standing, a faithful ally bound to the U.S. by a mutual defense treaty and a steadfast combatant in the battle for freedom. What has happened is agonizing and dismaying. We have been compelled to strive steadily harder to achieve self-reliance in a world situation which is so difficult and treacherous. Now we can perceive the true meaning of the late President Chiang Kai-shek's instruction. The late President told us that "under all conditions only our own strength is real strength" and that "we must lay the foundations of any enterprise for ourselves and also resolve all the problems involved by ourselves. As a consequence, we have never been depressed nor discouraged. On the contrary, we have become more determined than ever to brace up and continue the struggle for national survival and the development of our people.

Once diplomatic relations had been severed, the two countries conducted negotiations which had no parallel of style or substance in the history of diplomacy. We were completely aware that the negotiation environment was ominous in the extreme. But we had no choice except to restrain ourselves, enduring humiliation and "upholding our target and holding our temper in check" so as to make sure of attaining our national goal. We were deeply aware of the heavy burden that rested on our shoulders, yet realized that we had to exert ourselves and overcome all difficulties in the national interest. Our only choice was to take up the burden courageously and endure all hardships in order to protect the lives, freedom and happiness of the 17 million people in this bastion of national revival, and at the same time help our hundreds of millions of compatriots on the mainland throw off the yoke of Communist tyranny and come to enjoy with us a life of freedom and happiness. This is an immense responsibility involving the destiny of generation upon generation of the Chinese people. It is necessary that we have unconquerable determination and take up the burden and fulfill our task. Thus our enduring of humiliation is by no means a sign of cowardice or weakness. Rather, it is a manifestation of courage and fortitude. At the same time, our endurance of humiliation also has a limit, because we know that only when the Republic of China stands erect—upright and firm—can the peace and stability of East Asia be assured. We have therefore adhered steadfastly to the five negotiation principles of "continuity," "reality," "security," "legality" and "governmentality." We did so for the common interests of the two countries and the happiness of

Asia and the whole world. We have accepted this virtue as our burden and tried hard to minimize the hurt to open a new page in the book of history. In this time we should serve as witnesses for history and also as its creators.

During the last four months, many developments seem to have promised major apocalyptical imprints for future history.

First, our people at home and abroad have shown their soaring patriotism and wholehearted support of the government with enthusiastic and touching deeds. Scene after scene of moving stories have coalesced into page upon page of a patriotic panorama revealing the unanimous anti-Communist determination of the Chinese people and attesting that the tighter the crunch of the moment, the more solidly united are the people in showing the invincible spirit of the Chinese race.

Second, the U.S. Congress and huge numbers of Americans have extended to us their unparalleled warm friendship and massive support, providing unmistakable evidence that justice is always to be found in the hearts of the people and that the relationship between the Republic of China and the United States is indivisible. We are deeply appreciative and increasingly confident that ties between the two countries will be further developed and made even stronger.

We can also see that during this same period our enslaved compatriots on the mainland have emerged like winds and clouds to cry out for freedom, democracy, jobs and especially for the emulation of Taiwan. This anti-Communist uproar, which has been swelling up in the hearts of our mainland compatriots for years, is convincing evidence that they are hungry for liberty and prosperity and that they have maintained their allegiance to our government. These developments also show the great influence that the bastion of national revival on Taiwan, Penghu, Kinmen and Matsu is exercising over changes in the mainland situation.

Also of particular note during this period were drastic changes occurring in other parts of the world. These included the armed clashes between the Vietnamese Communists and Cambodian Communists, the Chinese Communist military action in Vietnam, convulsive changes in the political picture from the Middle East to Iran, disintegration of the Central Treaty Organization, conflict between South Yemen and North Yemen, war and turmoil in Africa and the expansion of the Communist shadow into the Indian Ocean. These developments are either a result of the competitive expansion of the Chinese Communists and the Soviet Union in their struggle for power and hegemony, or a demonstration of Communist bellicosity and tyranny carried out against innocent people. These occurrences also show why the Chinese Communist regime is not helpful to world peace but, on the contrary has directly or indirectly added to the crises and perils of the world.

Without doubt, the situation of the world is changing for the worse.

For our part, we adhere to principle in our course of conduct. This means that we stick to our revolutionary guidelines, persist in our anti-Communist position amidst these drastic changes and display to the full our great staying power in implementing basic policy despite all turmoils. We have an established line of priority in our struggle. This is to seek survival and stability first, then to strive for expansion and development, and finally to go forward to victory and success. Given our unfaltering diligence and buoyant spirits and the determination to contribute our wisdom and our hearts, we are convinced that we can move out along firm ground in accordance with this understanding and strategy and be assured of winning.

Looking over the world situation, we are certain that the pivotal position of the Republic of China is even more important than at any time in the past. The Chinese people on the mainland are sure that Communism is going to fall. They are disenchanted with Chinese Communist hypocrisy and deception and have lost all their illusions about the regime. They have come to understand that the existence of the Republic of China represents the hope of achieving China's destiny. Their only aspiration is to see the strength that they observe in our bastion of national recovery employed in the early recovery of the mainland. Under such circumstances, we must clench our teeth, endure any further buffeting, stand firm and break through any adverse tide by continuing our endeavors to make the country more powerful and our strength greater in order to carry out the tasks that our mainland compatriots expect of us.

In fact, our efforts to implement our policy of democratic government, a free economy and an open society have given rise to a powerful shock wave on the mainland and penetrated deeply into the hearts of our compatriots there. This equates to the landing of our forces on the mainland and has brought about the welling up of an angry anti-Communist tide. We are supremely confident of continuing this course and are certain that the mainland dawn will soon be here.

Assuredly, our principal task of today is the strengthening of this bastion of national revival. We must close ranks and mount strict guard against the enemy's infiltration, schism and subversion. All of these are malicious tricks of the Chinese Communists, who concentrate on trying to "divide one into two" so as to trick and weaken us by creating contradictions in our ranks. Each of us must be vigilant against this enemy conspiracy and realize that we share the same fate, like passengers aboard a boat. We must exhibit our team spirit of "combining two into one" and "forging ten thousand souls into one." With one will and one body, we then can frustrate the Chinese Communist intention of "dividing one into two" and defeat the united front.

Our ancient sages told us to prepare for danger when we were safe. Today we lack even safety, and have reason to maintain our vigilance at the highest possible level. When the enemy finds that his united front endeavors are futile, he may well take the risk of attempting the forceful invasion of Taiwan. This means that we must complete our preparations to meet such a challenge. However, I want to affirm that if the Chinese Communists should actually employ armed force against us, this would mark the beginning of their total collapse and serve as the opportunity for our victory. I should like to offer the "liberation army" this sincere advice at this time: All of you are Chinese sons by blood. Unfortunately, the Chinese Communists have enslaved you and made you their tools. You had better rise up and liberate our mainland compatriots rather than serving as the cannon fodder of the Chinese Communist chieftains in human seas warfare. You had better rally under the Flag of Blue Sky and White Sun, serving as volunteers of the Three Principles of the People and destroying the filthy and ugly five-starred Communist banner. In this way you can respond behind the enemy's lines to the counterattack launched by the National Revolutionary Army, eradicate tyrannical Communist rule and restore freedom to each and every one of our people.

Time after time we have reiterated that we shall never reconcile ourselves with the evil of Communism, and that sustained by the strength of our democracy, freedom and open political and economic construction, we shall march to the mainland and save China from a destiny of doom. We shall never relax in this struggle until the glorious Flag of Blue Sky and White Sun illumines the whole of China and the benevolent rule of the Three Principles of the People is restored to all of the Chinese.

"We shall return to the mainland."

# Dialogue with Jose V. Colchero, Reporter, *Ya,* Madrid, Spain

*April 20, 1979*

*Q1. Do you consider the U.S. severance of diplomatic relations as a betrayal by the United States, which has been the ally of your country for the last 30 years?*

A. There have been worldwide reports and editorial comments to the effect that the United States severed diplomatic relations with the Republic of China and thereby betrayed a faithful ally and yielded completely to the Chinese Communists' terms. International judgment of this matter indicates that many of our friends support our position; they have spoken of their innermost feelings in communicating with us. I would prefer not to say more on this subject.

*Q2. Severance of diplomatic relations between the United States and the Republic of China has defined Taiwan's position in its relationship with other countries. Do you think the countries having diplomatic relations with Peiping will maintain increasingly substantial relations with your country?*

A. The basic national policy of the Republic of China is to maintain and strengthen its relations with all freedom-loving democratic countries.

*Q3. Do you think the Chinese-Vietnamese conflict will threaten Asian peace or is it a necessary action of the Chinese nation in resisting foreign aggression?*

A. The conflict between the Chinese and Vietnamese Communists is a struggle between Asian Communist regimes and should not be mistaken as a national war of

resistance. With its cultural background and racial traits, the Chinese nation can undertake all-people resistance against the invasion of a neighbor but will never bully a smaller nation. The Chinese Communists are undertaking actions contrary to Chinese tradition.

*Q4. Any understanding between Peiping and Washington will upset the traditional balance of alliances. Is there any possibility that Taipei will approach Moscow?*

A. This is an absolute impossibility.

*Q5. Can your country maintain powerful armed forces in the absence of the U.S. provision of weapons?*

A. National defense capability is not wholly dependent upon a country's weapons. Confidence and the will to defend freedom are even more important. We have unmatched confidence and the will to protect our free way of life. Most of the weapons and equipment required by our armed forces are made at home and we are also developing the capability to produce modern armaments.

*Q6. Your country is strongly anti-Communist and declines conciliation with Communists. However, the world trend is toward "peaceful coexistence" of differing political systems. Could it be that your anti-Communism is a serious mistake?*

A. Peace cannot be won by forsaking principle and yielding one's fundamental position. Conciliation without principle can only bring inescapable catastrophe to any country and to the world. The

appeasement of Munich is a lesson the world should never forget. I sincerely hope that no leader of today's free world will repeat such a mistake.

*Q7. Teng Hsiao-ping s pragmatism prevails on the Chinese mainland. Do you think this will bring Taipei and Peiping into contact, accelerate the independence of Taiwan or result in an autonomous position like that of Hongkong or Macao?*

A. None of these surmises is possible. The historic mission of the Republic of China is to help the 800 million compatriots on the Chinese mainland regain their freedom and enjoy the same affluence and well-being as the people of free China. Until this mission is accomplished, we shall never give up our principle of struggle. We shall adhere to our goal so as not to disappoint our compatriots.

*Q8. Spain has been a faithful friend of the Republic of China. What kind of relationship do you think should be maintained between our countries?*

A. Our countries have a long history and great cultures. The people of our countries uphold freedom and democracy and pursue lives of well-being. Based on these common ideals, our two peoples should develop closer relations based on economic, trade and cultural cooperation.

Jose V. Colchero came from *Ya* of Madrid. President Chiang told him that the Republic of China wanted to develop closer economic and cultural relations with the Spanish people and government.

# Dialogue with Marsh Clark, Southeast Asia Bureau Chief, Time Magazine

*May 3, 1979*

*Q1. For some years you and your people had a nightmare about normalization of U.S.-Communist Chinese relations. Has the reality proved as bad as the dream?*

A. We did everything possible to prevent that nightmare from actually taking place. However, it did occur. The first task for us was to face the reality and to manage the crisis imposed upon the nation, especially the adverse effects on the society. We had to do something to minimize the unfortunate consequences. In the past months we have been doing everything possible to strengthen this society — economically, socially, militarily, and politically — and we have been taking every possible step to unite the country. We feel that only with internal solidarity can we meet the external blow.

Aside from the steps that we have been taking to meet the challenge, we know that the Repub-

lic of China and the United States share many, many common interests and that close people-to-people relations between our two countries will never be terminated.

*Q2. In the days following the announcement of derecognition, your stock market dropped 15 per cent. Today it has rebounded and is 11 per cent higher than it was on Dec. 16. Is that not a sign of confidence both domestically and internationally in Taiwan's future?*

A. If I were to say that the change of relations between the United States and the Republic of China has had no damaging effect at all on the Republic of China, that would be wrong. There has been some damage to the Republic of China during the past few months. In particular, there are still people in this country who feel hurt psychologically.

At the end of this year the Sino-American Mutual Defense Treaty will come to an end, and that will become another key element in our relations.

The Republic of China should do everything possible to meet the new challenge. The two weeks after Dec. 16 was the most unstable period. But after the government announced some decisive measures to meet the challenge, the situation became more stabilized.

During that two-week period the stock market dropped and the exchange rate between the US dollar and the NT dollar on the black market rose. And domestic and foreign investors seemed to be reconsidering their investments in the Republic of China.

But it seems to us that since January the situation has improved greatly and is now quite stable. In managing the crisis, the first two weeks were the toughest period.

*Q3. Are you reassured by the terms of the Taiwan Relations Act passed by Congress and signed by President Carter? Are there not some provisions of the legislation that give you even broader protection than ever before, for instance against economic boycott or blockade (by the P.R.C.)?*

A. I feel that the Sino-American Mutual Defense Treaty was important to the Republic of China and also to the United States. In particular, when we look back at the time — in 1954 — when we signed the treaty with the United States — and I was involved in the negotiating process leading up to the treaty — it was clear that the United States felt the need for some kind of security arrangement. When we compare the situation in 1954 and that of 1978, there doesn't seem to have been much change, especially in terms of the American defense posture in this part of the world.

For the good of the United States as well as of the Republic of China, this treaty should be kept in effect. But the United States has decided to terminate it and President Carter has already announced his intention to terminate at the end of this year.

Now Congress has passed an Act saying that the United States continues to be concerned about

the security of the Republic of China. I think that's something that's necessary. The United States must remain concerned about the security and stability of the Republic of China because that is

very important in terms of the U.S. strategic position in this part of the world. The purpose of the Mutual Defense Treaty was exactly in that context.

I want to emphasize that when the Vietnam War was over, people talked about the so-called domino theory. If something serious happened in the Taiwan Straits and the U.S. lost its presence in this part of the world, then the damage to the security of the world would be much more serious than the fall of Vietnam — and it would cause serious defense problems to Japan, the Philippines, Singapore and other countries in the region.

An important interview carried around the world by Time was based on the questions asked by Marsh Clark of the magazine's Southeast Asia Bureau. The interview was accompanied by an article on ROC progress.

*Q4. In the new situation, are you satisfied that Taiwan will be able to defend itself against attack?*

A. When we talk about the defense of Taiwan, we shouldn't just confine our thinking to the military area. War in the Taiwan Straits would be of such scope as to involve political as well as military actions and movements. So we should not confine our thinking to strength only in the military sense, but also political considerations.

As far as the Republic of China is concerned, we have 17 million people, all of them concerned about their future, all of them peace-loving and trying very hard to preserve freedom and stability here. If any crisis should occur, they would unite to counter the challenge. That political solidarity and zeal to preserve our freedom would add to our military strength.

To consider the other side, Communist China, if they were to take military action against us, many people there would oppose it and it would lead to the development of anti-war movement and perhaps even a civil war. That possibility will prevent the Communists from taking military action against Taiwan.

So we shouldn't just consider the military balance — how many airplanes and how many ships on this side and that side — but must also consider the political elements that would affect the situation.

On the one hand, we need American manufactured weapons.

On the other hand, we want to manufacture our own weapons. We would therefore have dual sources of supply in terms of our military requirements.

The military strength on the mainland may increase from day to day, so our capability must also increase to meet the challenge from the other side. In the future, we want to be more self-reliant in weapons supply.

We are also pleased to see that the U.S. is still concerned about Taiwan's stability and security. That gives us a feeling of confidence psychologically.

*Q5. You said just now that the possibility of internal strife on the mainland would deter Peking from attacking Taiwan. There was no such problem when the Chinese Communists recently invaded Vietnam. There was no discernable anti-war movement as such. I take it that you believe it is one thing for China to attack Vietnam, but it would be quite another for Chinese to go to war against fellow Chinese?*

A. Yes, war between the Communist Chinese regime and the Vietnamese regime is quite different in nature from war between the Chinese Communist regime and the Republic of China.

When they took military action against Vietnam, the Chinese Communists could find many excuses to justify it. But if they go to war against us, they would have to have a very good reason.

This has to be looked at from a Chinese perspective. When the

Republic of China was making a decision on nuclear matters, we adopted a firm policy not to manufacture any nuclear weapons. If we were to possess nuclear weapons, what would we use them for? Our only enemy is the Chinese Communist regime. But we don't want to kill any of our Chinese compatriots.

If they dare to start any military action against the Republic of China, it would start a new political crisis on the mainland. You may recall what happened in 1958 at the time of the Chinese Communist bombardment of the offshore island of Quemoy. They never even tried to invade the island, but it still caused some internal political trouble on the mainland. Peng Teh-huai was removed from office because of some differing policy assessments.

Also, Vietnam and China are contiguous by land, but when you talk about military action between the mainland and Taiwan, you must consider the natural barrier between us — the Taiwan Straits — which is 100 miles at its narrowest and 120 miles at the broadest point.

If they undertake such amphibious action, it would be a very risky enterprise on their part. They would have to be prepared to sacrifice one million, two million or even three million people in that action. It would also involve a great logistical and transport problem for them.

But for our part, we can't simply rely on such assumptions for our safety, but must take all possible precautions. Our national defense policy places top priority on air and naval strength in order to defend the Taiwan Straits. And that's why we stress air and naval equipment when we seek to purchase military supplies from the United States.

*Q6. Do you not consider that Peking's preoccupation with Vietnam, Cambodia and the Soviet Union and also with the "four modernizations" lessens the threat of an attack on Taiwan from the mainland?*

A. According to our understanding, the Chinese Communist military action against Vietnam, caused more casualties than Communist China first expected. They had, according to our information, more than 30,000 killed or wounded, which was many more than they had anticipated. They thought they would have an easy time moving into Vietnam, but in fact it turned out not to be so easy.

Talking with an American visitor, Communist Chinese vice premier Li Hsien-nien mentioned that the military action was not an end to the conflict with Vietnam but rather the beginning of a long, protracted involvement. If Vietnam becomes more stabilized and if Vietnam, Cambodia and Laos become a base for Soviet power in the area, I don't think the Chinese Communists would just sit with their hands folded.

It is a complicated situation and there is no easy solution to the problem (of Hanoi-Peking relations). The negotiations going on now are less peace talks than war talks.

As to the "four modernizations," the Chinese Communists themselves understand that it won't be easy to achieve such an ambitious venture. Why, then, did they announce such an ambitious program? The purpose was simply to fool the Americans and other foreigners — to attract their attention. The same is true of the "big character posters" on Democracy Wall. The "four modernizations" were designed to give the outside world the impression that the mainland was going to turn into a huge market.

Regarding the posters, Teng was not trying to foster a real democratic movement but only wanted a show window so that foreigners would believe that mainland China was becoming more democratized and modernized. But, in fact, no country can be modernized unless it can first modernize its thinking and its political system. Unless Communist China modernizes its thinking and its political system, it can never succeed with the "four modernizations." So I don't think the "four modernizations" can have any effect on us.

*Q7. Do you perceive any circumstances in the near or foreseeable future for improvement of relations with the mainland, any avenues for closening the ties? I am speaking of trade, postal exchange, and so on.*

A. No.

I would like to call the attention of our friends to the fact that any "contacts" or "ties" would just be a tool used by the Chinese Communists to undermine our psychological defense against

Communism. We don't want to help them undermine our own defenses.

*Q8. As regards the Olympics, the Republic of China has agreed to an arrangement of one China, two committees. Is this a sign that you are becoming more flexible?*

A. On the Olympic question, our guiding principle is that we are now a member country and we want to stay within the Olympic organization. A decision was made by the International Olympic Committee that they would have two committees — an Olympic Committee, Taipei and an Olympic Committee, Peking. That was their decision, not one made by us. Our policy is simply to preserve our membership in the International Olympic Committee, and it can't be interpreted that we have made a compromise on the issue of "one China."

*Q9. Outsiders have been impressed with the patriotism and cohesion on Taiwan after derecognition. I believe the public contributed out of the individuals' own pockets over US$84 million to an emergency defense fund. Has Washington-Peking normalization had, in fact, some positive aspects?*

A. The reason why we attach great significance to the donation campaign that you mentioned is not just the impressive figures, even though they are far beyond the government's expectations, but that so many ordinary citizens made contributions. There were many heartwarming and moving stories. For example, a cook who had saved up all his life to buy an expensive Omega watch donated the watch to the defense fund. In Hualien a city councilman donated all his property, even including his house. Some old ladies donated all their jewelry, and a taxi driver contributed a whole month's income. There were thousands of such moving stories, which touched me very much.

*Q10. When the U.S. announced normalization of relations with Peking, your government postponed local elections that were scheduled for the following week. Why was that done?*

A. The main reason why the election was postponed was not that the government couldn't have controlled the situation if the election had been held. But during an election campaign there must be many differences of opinion aired. We didn't want to see such arguments become a destabilizing force in our society. When stability has been fully restored, the elections will be held.

Among those campaigning were many who were very critical of the government. In the aftermath of the events of Dec. 16, those people might have been beaten up by patriotic crowds. We didn't want to see that happen.

*Q11. Isn't it true that you have still gone ahead with certain domestic reforms, such as a restructuring of the judiciary?*

A. Some reform measures have been adopted, including a reassignment of the judicial branch of government. Much of our administrative structure comes from traditional Chinese practice and were not 'creations of the Nationalist government. But now, because of new requirements and new demands, we will continue the Ministry of Justice under the executive branch but shift the court system to a separate branch.

*Q12. It has been four months since the American derecognition of Taiwan, and the dust has settled, so to speak. What impression or message do you wish now to convey to the world? Confidence, determination, optimism, unhappiness, despair, pessimism?*

A. I am always optimistic. My philosophy is that the more difficulties we encounter, the more we become united. As long as we work hard, we can overcome whatever difficulties we meet along the way.

In a speech I gave recently, I emphasized three points. The first thing we must do is to establish stability and ensure our survival. After that we can concentrate on development, and finally we will be able to attain victory.

Through your magazine I would like the American people to realize that their genuine, true friends are here, in this country. I have every confidence that we can continue our friendship with our American friends, and we will do everything possible on our part to deserve the confidence of the American people. There is a Chinese expression that no one can wield a knife to cut the ties between two close friends.

When I was a young man, I had a great teacher, Mr. Wu Chih-huei. When I complained about all the problems I faced, he responded: "What are you here for, if not to solve such problems?"

# A chronological
# list of
# documents